*An easy-to-understand guide to the incredible
product that may soon revolutionize your life*

Computers for use in the home are no longer limited to the
rich or the electronic hobbyist. Now virtually anyone can afford to buy his or her own computer to compute income taxes,
maintain personal records, calculate recipe quantities, teach
languages or other subjects, play sophisticated electronic
games, and perform dozens of other useful and exciting tasks.

HOME COMPUTERS: A MANUAL OF POSSIBILITIES is your best
guide to understanding, buying, and using your very own home
computer. It describes:

- what a computer actually is and does
- how computers count
- the "hardware" that is a part of every computer
- how you can program your own—or any—computer
- the kinds of games, programs, and applications available
  now
- how home computers will change your life in the very
  near future
- illustrated with over 50 explanatory drawings

Richard M. Koff is a licensed engineer, inventor, patent
holder, and author of HOW DOES IT WORK?, now in its twen-
tieth printing. He presently acts as management consultant to
publishers and other corporate executives and has a small computer at home which he programs to solve clients' problems.

HOME COMPUTERS

COMPUTERS

A MANUAL OF POSSIBILITIES

RICHARD M. KOFF

HARCOURT BRACE JOVANOVICH

NEW YORK AND LONDON

Library of Congress Cataloging in Publication Data

Koff, Richard M
    Home computers.

    1. Computers.   I. Title.
QA76.K539   001.6'4'04   78–53883
ISBN 0–15–142163–3

First edition

B   C   D   E

CONTENTS

PREFACE

Just as high-fidelity equipment started with component amplifiers, tuners, and turntables, so did the microcomputer start
with separate central processing units, memory boards, keyboards, teletypewriters, and television tube displays. In 1975
the first microcomputer components were produced and ea-
gerly bought by engineers and programmers who had worked
with big computers in their jobs and were delighted at the opportunity to have relatively inexpensive micros at home. These
hobbyists struggled to wire up often-mismatched components
and then used the machine to play simple, and later fairly sophisticated, games.

That it worked at all was reward enough. The hobbyist gets
as much fun, maybe more, out of wiring components together
and making them work as he does in actually using the computer to solve problems. It is important to him to know exactly
what goes into his computer in terms of hardware and what
sort of signals chase each other around the circuits. He will
take the position that if you don't know electronics and machine language, you can't really use the computer.

That isn't true and that is what this book is all about. In 1977 the first assembled, functioning computers for the home were offered in retail stores at prices close to that of a color television set. The buyer doesn't have to know anything about what goes on inside. He can concentrate on making the computer do whatever applications please him.

Computer people call this process of getting the computer to do a particular job "programming," and while the equipment for the home user today is well designed, powerful in its computational ability, and economical, the programming that manufacturers are supplying has a long way to go. A few games, a few educational courses, some simple home finance and menu-planning programs are available, but no one knows what users will want so we may just have to write our own programs until there are enough of us out here to make it a profitable venture for a courageous publisher.

Programming is more important than equipment. In this respect computers are like musical instruments. There is a lot to learn about the manufacture and functioning of, say, a violin. Wood structure, shape and finish, string materials, hardware, bow design, and rosin took hundreds of years to bring to their present state of perfection. But the making of the violin only sets the stage. Composers and performers make the music. So it is with computers. Without electronics, electromagnetics, solid-state transistors, radio, and telephone there could be no computer. Programmers and users are what make the music.

Like its subject, this book divides naturally into two parts. Part 1 (the first five chapters) tells you how computers work, where they came from, and where the equipment can be expected to go in the next ten years. Part 2 (the last five chapters) is concerned with how you talk to computers, how you program them, what they are doing for us now, and what we can expect them to be doing in the near future.

Between the two parts you will find a short summary and review chapter (Chapter 6) that takes a quick look at the various components, how they work together, what is necessary and what is optional to make a functioning system. I don't believe that you have to know every detail of a machine in order to use and enjoy it. But I *do* believe it is interesting and useful to know as much about these things as possible. So if you prefer, start with Part 2 and come back to the earlier chapters as curiosity moves you. They won't make a computer expert out of anyone, but they may go into more detail than you'll want initially with your new computer staring at you blankly from the dining room table. After the first excitement wears off and you begin to run into the limitations of a bare-bones computer, you will want to add more equipment, such as an additional memory unit or a remote controller or a telephone coupler. If that is the case, read Part 1 for guidance.

This is the start of a trip into a vast world of possibilities. It is a real-life real-world adventure. I am very glad you can come along.

PART 1

UNDERSTANDING
THE EQUIPMENT

1

AN INTRODUCTION
TO COMPUTERS

Sometime within the next twenty-four months you will stop at your favorite department store and pick up your own personal computer. It will be about the size of your color television set, cost less, and be more entertaining and more useful than just about anything else you own.

Twenty years ago only a company the size of General Motors could afford the million dollars it would cost to buy a computer no better than yours. It would comfortably fill a one-bedroom apartment, use enough electricity every day to heat a two-bedroom house for a month, and require enough service people to run a small hotel.

Thirty years ago even the national budget wouldn't have been able to pay for the computing power you will plug into your living room wall socket. When I graduated from engineering school in 1948, the digital computer was not even a feature in science fiction stories. Most families did not have television; there were no transistor radios, no jet airplanes, no atomic power stations, no artificial satellites, no pushbutton telephones. Air conditioning was a fan blowing through a wet screen and convertible cars had canvas tops. The only plastics were Bakelite and Cellophane, the only preserved foods were in cans or dried K-rations. The freezer of the refrigerator was for ice and ice cream—there were no frozen foods, microwave ovens, or plastic wrap.

The list is fascinating, not because of what we didn't have in 1948, but because we have so much more today. Everything on the list assists in some physical aspect of our lives—we can communicate faster, we can prepare gourmet foods with less trouble, we are cooler in the summer, warmer in the winter, and we wear clothes that take less effort to keep clean and looking new. Everything takes less effort, from brushing our teeth with an electric toothbrush to lighting a charcoal fire with an electric starter.

And now, for the first time, the average person can have a machine to increase his mental power in the same way that the electricity in his home has increased his muscle power. "Power" is one of the favorite words of computer people. It may seem absurd to think that just because a machine can add, subtract, multiply, or compare two numbers or words it can be considered powerful, but that is precisely what computer designers mean.

Much of the thinking we do involves arithmetic or logic: adding up a sales slip, expanding a recipe for a larger number of guests, computing interest on a mortgage or savings account, or planning a trip—all require simple arithmetical operations. Even more frequent are the little logical decisions we make each day: Should I put my right or left shoe on first? Shall I shower first or shave? Should I take the bus or drive? Do I have enough time to stop at the drugstore on the way to the office? Each decision has its own interior logic, a reason that is the result of an internal preference.

We make most such decisions so quickly we aren't aware of the mental processes involved. And if a machine is to be of any use to us it will have to operate with equal speed, which is why speed is one of the most important measures of computer power.

Let's take multiplication speed as our example because multiplication occurs so often in business and scientific areas and because it is so much a part of our everyday lives. In order to judge the computer's speed at multiplication we must first consider how fast a human can perform the same job. If you are good with numbers you can probably multiply two ten-digit numbers in about three minutes. The old-fashioned mechanical desk calculators can do it in about fifteen seconds. The modern computer can multiply in a fraction of a second.

Attaining that speed required a new use of mathematics and electric circuitry. The process began in the middle of the nineteenth century when Charles Babbage first dreamed up and started construction of his "Analytical Engine." He was never to finish the machine and it is obvious now that he had no idea how difficult a task he had set for himself. But the principles of operation are similar to those of today's computers. His machine was based on the idea of using pure numbers in the computer rather than measured quantities. To fully understand this we have to know the difference between a "digital" computer and an "analog" computer.

ANALOG COMPUTERS

When you want to know what the outdoor temperature is, you look at a mercury thermometer. The thermometer is a thin tube of glass with a large bulb at the bottom. Mercury fills the bulb and runs part way up the tube. Along the side or under the tube is a scale that reads in even divisions, say, from minus forty to plus one hundred degrees Fahrenheit. As the temperature rises, the mercury expands in volume and rises up the tube. When the temperature drops, the mercury contracts and sinks back down the tube toward the bulb. The temperature reading is therefore a measure of the distance the mercury has traveled along the scale; that is, it is an "analog" of the temperature of the mercury.

There are hundreds of analogs in our world. The speedometer of your car, the fuel gauge, the radio dial, a clock face with hour and minute hands, all read the distance of a pointer along or around a scale. By analogy they tell you the amount of gasoline in your tank, the frequency to which the radio is tuned, the time of day.

Until fairly recently almost all our measurements were made by analogy. Temperature, pressure, time, speed, loudness, electric current or voltage were measured by devices that transformed what we really wanted to know into a proportional electric current, and then that current was used to swing a pointer around a dial. Then engineers discovered that currents could be added, subtracted, or used to modify each other in such a way that they would represent mathematical equations. Because they were constructed with such circuits, the first computers were called analog computers.

Unfortunately, the early analog computers required large amounts of electric power and hundreds of miles of wire. Furthermore, they were very specialized—an analog computer used to aim a gun was no good for navigating a ship, and it certainly couldn't be used to figure a payroll. And finally, their applications were limited because their measurements were only approximations of physical states. Businessmen couldn't use them to maintain precise records of accounts or inventories. Nor could some of the physical sciences such as astronomy, which deals with distances so huge that a small error could mean the difference between finding a particular star in the telescope's field of view or wasting a whole night's viewing.

DIGITAL COMPUTERS

Then in the early years of World War II, IBM and Harvard University collaborated in the construction of the first digital computer. Like Babbage's Analytical Engine, the computer manipulated numbers, not quantities like electric current or voltage. The numbers were stored on counters like the one measuring off miles on your automobile dashboard. The IBM computer contained 72 counters in which 23-digit numbers were stored. There were hundreds of switches to set constants and the computer was controlled ("programmed," in current terminology) by a punched paper tape.

The counter is a mechanical device, which means it has moving parts—metal rings driven by shafts and gears—that are slowed by friction and by the very effort it takes to get them moving. This puts an upper limit on the computational speed that can be expected from such a computer. In terms of multiplication power this machine could multiply two 10-digit numbers in about three seconds.

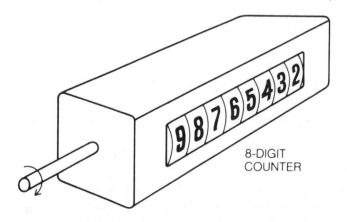

8-DIGIT
COUNTER

At the same time Bell Laboratories was building a computer which used telephone-type relays rather than counters to store numbers. In a relay an electric current is sent through a coil of wire surrounding a soft iron core. The core is magnetized by the current and attracts the toggle of a switch. The toggle moves contacts either open or closed and keeps the contacts in that position until the current is cut off. In this way the relay "remembers" and maintains its position, in the same way that the counter remembers and maintains its

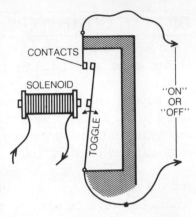

position. The relay counts by twos—"OFF" is zero, "ON" is one—but, as we will see in the next chapter, it can be used to calculate as well as, if not better than, the ten-position counter.

The Bell Laboratories machine could multiply two ten-digit numbers in one second. That was pretty fast—sixty multiplications in a minute—but even at that speed there was no way the machine could be used for practical accounting applications. For example, the weekly payroll for a company with 1,-000 employees requires at least five or six calculations per employee: the number of hours worked multiplied by the wage rate, a deduction for insurance, another for Social Security, and a percentage for federal, state, and local taxes. In a computer the numbers have to do a lot of moving around as well—each employee's hours and salary and other information have to be looked up and brought into the place where the arithmetic actually takes place. The results have to be stored somewhere else. So to figure the payroll of a thousand employees the Bell Labs machine, even at one second per multiplication function, would take three or four days.

For many engineering or scientific problems the number of multiplications is much higher. A weather report would take over three hundred days on the Bell Labs machine. To get the speeds that would allow for a 24-hour forecast the computer can't use counters or relays: it has to be totally electronic. It takes at least five-thousandths of a second to open or close the contacts of a relay. If the computer could be made totally electronic, the time necessary to move electrons through the various circuit elements would be in the order of one-millionth of a second—five thousand times faster than relay circuits.

To reach these speeds scientists and engineers decided to use vacuum tubes as their "counters."

A vacuum tube is a small envelope of glass from which all air has been evacuated. Four essential metal parts make up the circuit elements: a filament, a metal tube called a cathode, a grid, and a plate. The filament is like that in a standard light bulb. It glows hot when current is passed through it and heats the cathode which throws off a cloud of negatively charged electrons. The grid acts as a screen between the cathode and the plate. When the grid has a positive electric charge relative to the filament it attracts the negatively charged electrons, some of which pass right through the grid and hit the plate. Thus a flow of current goes from the cathode to the plate. On the other hand, when the grid has a negative charge relative to the cathode, the cloud of electrons is repelled and none reach the plate at all.

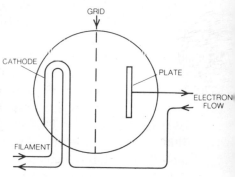

The speed of this starting and stopping is similar to that of all electron motions—close to the speed of light. This means that a change in the grid voltage level can cut off the flow of electrons to the plate in less than a billionth of a second.

The first all-electronic digital computer used vacuum tubes instead of counters or relays. In fact, ENIAC (for Electronic Numerical Integrator and Computer) had almost 18,000 vacuum tubes plus about 70,000 resistors, 10,000 capacitors, and 6,000 switches. It stood 10 feet high, 100 feet long, and 3 feet deep. In rows it filled a room 20 feet by 40 feet and consumed 140,000 watts of electric power when turned "on." If any one of the 18,000 tubes failed, the computer made mistakes. Thus the failure rate of any single tube had to be practically zero. The vacuum tubes were operated far below their capacity and tubes were bought which were supposed to last for 2,500 hours. Even so, ENIAC went "down" with tube failure every other day. However, ENIAC made another large step upward in speed; it could multiply two ten-digit numbers in three-thousandths of a second.

ENIAC was completed and operational at the end of 1945, but even before it was turned on for the first time, its successor had been designed and was in the process of being built. EDVAC (Electronic Discrete Variable Computer) had only 3,000 vacuum tubes and had a much larger memory. Its designers did this by an ingenious use of something called a delay line. Electrical pulses in a timed sequence are applied to one

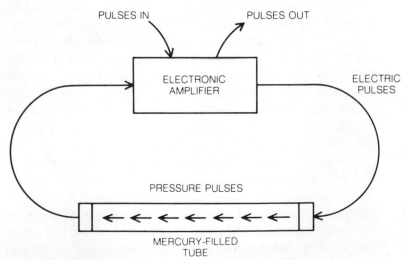

end of a long tube filled with mercury where they are transformed into pressure pulses. These pressure pulses take time to run to the tube's other end where they are sensed, transformed into electric pulses again, and sent back at the speed of light through a wire to the first end. And so on, around and around in a loop. A fairly long string of pulses (or the absence of pulses) can be kept cycling around this loop and read out or changed as needed. EDVAC had more number storage capacity than ENIAC and could multiply two ten-digit numbers in about one-thousandth of a second.

Both ENIAC and EDVAC were developed at the University of Pennsylvania with government grants. After the war it was evident that further support would have to come either from the academic community or from industry. The next machine was built at the Institute for Advanced Studies in Princeton. Many of the same inventors took part in the design of the IAS machine, and it made another leap forward—a multiplication could now be done in about half a thousandth of a second. The machine contained only 2,000 vacuum tubes.

From this point on computers became industrial products developed by such companies as Bell Laboratories, Burroughs, General Electric, International Business Machines, and Sperry Rand. The first all-electronic IBM machine was called the Selective Sequence Electronic Calculator and was installed at IBM headquarters on Madison Avenue in New York in January 1948. With this machine IBM launched itself into the computer business as a commercial venture distinct from its calculators and punch card machines. By 1953 IBM had introduced its now famous 701 which was soon followed by the 702, the 704 and 705, and the smaller 650.

Suddenly everyone was talking about electronic "brains" which would replace the human brain for almost everything. The computer could deal with large numbers of numbers, keep tabs on what belonged to what, do the simple addition and multiplication needed to produce company profit-and-loss statements and do it so fast and accurately that human accountants couldn't come close to competing. Banks found them wonderful for keeping track of the millions of checks they had to handle; airline companies used them for reservations; department stores and credit card companies used them to keep track of customer accounts and for monthly billing; television stations used them to predict the outcome of presidential elections.

ENTER THE TRANSISTOR

Still, the computer of the fifties was crude by today's standards. It took the invention of the transistor to change it from the elaborate and expensive business machine affordable only by the largest corporations, to standard office equipment for most companies, and, finally, to a home appliance.

A transistor is the equivalent of a vacuum tube, except it takes a tiny fraction of the electric power, the space, and the cost. A transistor permits or cuts off current between two zones on a crystal. Wires to the zones conduct current or not depending on an electric signal brought in by a third wire. Transistors have been combined in Integrated Circuits in which dozens and even hundreds of transistors are placed on the surface of a single crystal, and these in turn are now being replaced by Large Scale Integrated Circuits and by Very Large Integrated Circuits in which a million or more transistors are microscopically embedded on one quarter-inch square of crystal.

Consider the difference—ENIAC with 10,000 vacuum tubes filled a room the size of a basketball court and your personal computer has a million transistors on a chip you might lose between your fingers if you aren't careful.

We'll be talking about the various parts of your computer in later chapters—what is inside the machine and how it is made to work for you. Right now I'd like to talk a little about the place where you and your computer actually interact—the keyboard and screen or printer where the characters appear.

THE COMPUTER TERMINAL

Most home computers have a keyboard very much like that of an ordinary typewriter, with a few special buttons and a few more symbols. The keyboard will have a full set of alphabetical letters, ten digits, punctuation marks, a plus (+), minus (−), asterisk (*), and so on. It may have lowercase as well as capital letters if it is to be used for writing letters to friends or business associates.

Each time you press one of the typewriter keys you are giving the computer a one-character message. This is "input." The computer recognizes the character and will then display it on one of two types of "output" devices to let you know that it has received the message. The cathode ray tube (CRT) is an adaptation of a television picture tube. Lines of letters or numbers appear written in white or green against the black background of the screen. The advantage of the cathode ray tube is the high speed with which the characters can be displayed. At normal computer speeds that means the full screen of text—as many as 24 lines of 80 characters per line or 1,920 characters—can be written on the screen in about one second. This is a lot faster than you can read it. Also it consumes no paper or ink. The disadvantage of the cathode ray tube is that there is no permanent record of what was displayed, and once the screen has been filled, every additional line added at the bottom will displace a line off the top of the screen.

The second kind of computer output is an adaptation of the electric typewriter and it gives a permanent copy of the communication. The maximum speed of an IBM Selectric is around 15 characters per second. This is a lot slower than the cathode ray tube and almost unacceptable for computer applications. Most computer "printers" can operate at 30 characters per second and many can print a full line of 80 characters in less than a tenth of a second, but these printers are considerably more specialized and expensive.

The combination of an input keyboard plus an output cathode ray tube display or printer is called a terminal because it is your end of the line of communication with the computer. A terminal is as necessary for a personal computer as it is for large business or scientific computers. You see computer terminals at the check-in counter of airlines and at bank teller windows. Credit card companies confirm your credit rating at a cathode ray tube terminal so that the stored names and numbers are instantly visible and can be updated anytime.

TIME-SHARING

The terminal part of your personal computer will communicate with large-size computers as easily as small ones. I am not suggesting you buy a large computer, but you can rent time on one. You do this with a standard home telephone. You dial the proper number and then put the receiver in a gadget with two rubber cups that match the two ends of the phone handset. The electric signals from your terminal are transformed into sound tones that go through the telephone system to a distant computer which will then solve your problem or look up some information for you and send it back through the phone lines to be displayed on your screen. Large computers are so powerful that few users can keep them occupied for more than a split second at a time. Instead the computer is hooked up to dozens or even hundreds of users at the same time. It devotes itself to each user's problem in turn, solves it, and sends back an answer. While the user sits there absorbing his answer, the computer goes on to the next customer and works on his problem. This is called "time-sharing."

Computer time-sharing offers many things that personal, stand-alone computers can't ever do. It is much more than speed. After all, you are limited as to how fast messages can be sent through telephone lines. However, a time-sharing com-

puter can store whole libraries of programs and information—
much more memory than any individual user would ever need.
When you want a particular piece of data it would be easy to
call up the computer and have it find the answer in a few seconds. Also, the information can be kept up-to-date—up-to-the-
minute actually. For example, you can check supermarket sales
which the local supermarket manager has called or typed into
the computer center that morning from his terminal. You can
purchase a piece of furniture or an appliance that has been
listed in a computer-managed catalog. Classified ads can be
placed in the central computer memory bank, and when you
are looking for a specific item you can display everything in
that category. Terminals and time-sharing also offer the possibility of communicating with other users for a chess game or
bridge tournament among players who live miles apart.

COMPUTER LANGUAGES

The computer doesn't talk English. It is going to take a little
study to learn its language and logical structure. At the very
least you are going to have to learn how to turn it on and off
and get it doing whatever job you have for it. As you explore
new tasks that haven't already been prepared by others, you
will want to do some instruction writing (programming) of
your own. While there has been a lot of standardization of language and grammar, there is still a way to go. Each home computer has its own specific set of instructions in the same way
that each high fidelity set has its own knobs and switches. The
functions to be performed are much the same, but for the moment there is the usual confusion among manufacturers' standards. Eventually the industry will be narrowed down to the
few leaders who will settle on a single control language.

WHAT WILL IT DO?

When we talk about language it reminds me of the critical
question asked by anyone getting ready to buy a home com-

puter: "What can I use it for?" The usual answer is, "Anything you like." Which is about as helpful as the psychiatrist who tells his patients not to worry so much.

There are dozens of prewritten programs available right now that will do a particular job, teach a particular course, or play a particular game. Many business programs have been adapted for home uses such as budgeting, tax computations, recipes, and menu and diet calculations. A wonderfully promising area is in the educational field for home study of everything from mathematics to law, from English literature to religion.

Not everything promised by the enthusiast is likely to be available at the corner bookstore this Christmas. The burglar alarm program that will recognize your voice and habit patterns and control the houselights and door locks isn't quite that reliable yet and, even more important, the control of door locks and lights requires wiring that most homes don't have. Until there are totally wired houses, we can't expect to see the computer-controlled house. And it makes little sense to use your general-purpose educational and game-playing computer to control the timing on your microwave oven or the defrost cycle of your refrigerator. With integrated circuit chips costing just a dollar or two, why tie up a $600 computer for these menial tasks? A chip or two can be put into any appliance that needs one. And why pay to put wiring between the computer and every appliance in the house?

But maybe we are working too hard to justify the miracle. Isn't it enough if you can play a game like *Startrek*, study a course in dress design, fill out your 1040 tax form on April 15, recalculate Grandmother's favorite casserole recipe for a party of twenty, write a letter to a friend, maintain your Christmas card list, and print out all the envelopes in an hour?

Now to the task of learning what's inside that miracle and how to make more happen.

2

HOW COMPUTERS COUNT

After twelve school years of traditional arithmetic it is something of a jolt to learn that our number system may not be the best way to count. This system—which is called the "base-ten" system because it is based on nine numbers and zero—probably evolved because human beings come with ten fingers and ten toes. It's easy to count on our fingers, and this therefore seems the most logical system. But if anything, the base-ten system is one of the poorer systems for multiplication and division. Other systems, such as base-twelve or base-sixteen arithmetic, have substantial advantages for mental arithmetic. But, for reasons we'll see later, computers use base-two arithmetic and while you don't really have to know how the computer moves numbers around or what kind of numbers they are, they are so much a part of the power of the computer you might like to take a few minutes to learn how the base-two system works and how the computer uses it.

We'll start by being very clear about the difference between "digits" and "numbers." A *digit* is a single *number* in a particular place. In the base-ten system there is a units digit, a tens digit, a hundreds digit, and so on. Each digit may take the form of any one of the ten numbers 0 through 9. But that is true only for the base-ten system. In a base-eight system the digit takes the form of any one of eight numbers 0 through 7. In a base-sixteen system the digit takes the form of any one of sixteen numbers 0 through 9 plus A, B, C, D, E, F—or some other symbols for the numbers 10 through 15. In a base-two system, only two numbers per digit are used—0 and 1.

The base-two system is most suited to electronic computers because each digit requires a storage device of some kind and the storage device must be able to take as many states or positions as there are numbers. This "hardware" is much more complex and slower if the computer has to put a light through ten different brightnesses or magnetize a bit of iron to ten different magnetic strengths than if it has to take only two states. With only a 0 or a 1 (or "on" and "off") the circuitry can be much simpler and the computer can work at much greater speeds: at the speed of light, in fact. That is why electronic computers use the base-two system or a simple variation of it.

COUNTING

Since the methods of any arithmetic base are the same, it is probably best to review how they operate by using the familiar base-ten system as an example. How do we count in base-ten arithmetic? Starting with 0 (a very important number), we count:

0
1
2
3
4
5
6

7
8
9

at which point we run out of numbers. When all ten have been used we go back to the starting point with the first digit but add or "carry" one into the second place or "tens" digit.

10
11
12
13
14

and so on.

What have we done? We have counted through each of our ten given digits and then bumped over into the next digit place, the "tens" place, and continued counting into the teens. When the second nine has been reached in the units digit we bump another into the tens, making it twenty, and go back to 0 in the units digit.

Now let's see how this method works with a different base—say base-eight:

0
1
2
3
4
5
6
7

After 7 we run out of numbers so we have to bump a 1 into the next place and return to 0 for the units.

10
11

12
13
14
15
16
17
20

The numbers 1 through 7 in the base-eight system are the same as those in the base-ten system, but the number 10 in the base-eight system is actually equivalent to 8 in the base-ten system. That's because after the number 7 you get the symbol 10. A comparison of the way we count in base-ten and base-eight is as follows:

Base-Ten	Base-Eight
0	0
1	1
2	2
3	3
4	4
5	5
6	6
7	7
8	10
9	11
10	12
11	13
12	14
13	15
14	16
15	17
16	20
17	21

This all seems confusing because we are using the same symbols in both systems, but they mean different things. The number 20 in base-ten would use all your fingers and your toes. In base-eight that same count would have to be represented by the symbol 24. (You won't need four extra toes!) In order to avoid confusion you must be sure what the arithmetic base is and remember that the meaning of the numerical symbols is always different for each base.

As we saw earlier, the computer has problems with base-ten and base-eight arithmetic. Fortunately, we can create a two-valued arithmetic as easily as base-ten or base-eight arithmetic. A base-two arithmetic or *binary* system, as it is usually called, has two numbers—0 and 1—rather than 10 or 8. Counting from 1 to 18 in the three bases is as follows:

Base-Ten	Base-Eight	Base-Two
0	0	0
1	1	1
2	2	10
3	3	11
4	4	100
5	5	101
6	6	110
7	7	111
8	10	1000
9	11	1001
10	12	1010
11	13	1011
12	14	1100
13	15	1101
14	16	1110
15	17	1111
16	20	10000
17	21	10001
18	22	10010

Because the base-two system uses only 0s and 1s, the difference in symbols is a lot more obvious. The base-two system runs out of numbers every two counts—much faster than base-eight or base-ten—so it adds new digits much more often than base-eight or base-ten. But with only two numbers to remember, the computer has a much easier time. The binary digit—a 0 or 1 in most printing systems—is called a "bit." Computers store bits, count with bits, and control with bits as we will see.

I'd like to show you how to add, subtract, multiply, and divide in this new arithmetic. The first time through we'll just follow the same rules we use for base-ten arithmetic. We'll review those rules briefly, but you'll see how easy it is once we have done it once or twice.

ADDITION

Suppose we want to add two base-ten numbers.

$$\begin{array}{r} 1357 \\ + 2468 \\ \hline \end{array}$$

We always start at the far right with the "least significant digit." It is least significant because it counts in ones. We add the least significant digits—the 7 and the 8—to get 15. We write the 5 in the least significant digit position of our answer and "carry" the 1—actually 10—to the second significant digit.

$$\begin{array}{r} 1357 \\ + 2468 \\ \hline 5 \text{ carry } 1 \end{array}$$

The next step is to add the two digits in the tens position—5 plus 6 is 11—and add to that the 1 carried over, making 12. We write the 2 and carry the remaining 1.

```
  1357
+ 2468
```
25 carry 1

Next we add the two digits in the hundreds position—3 plus 4 is 7—and add to that the 1 we carried over, making 8. This we write in and there is no digit to carry.

```
  1357
+ 2468
```
825

Finally we get to the most significant digit in the thousands position:

```
  1357
+ 2468
```
3825

and having run out of numbers we are finished.

Let's try the same thing with two binary numbers.

```
  110010110
+  10111011
```

We start with the least significant digit at the far right. Add 1 plus 0 and we get 1.

```
  110010110
+  10111011
```
1

There are no carries so we go to the next digit to the left. Now we have a problem. What is 1 plus 1 in the binary system? Well we know $1 + 1 = 2$, but there is no 2 in binary numbers. In this system $1 + 1 = 10$. (The comparable operation in the base-ten system is $9 + 1 = 10$.) So what we have to do here is write in the 0 and carry 1.

```
  110010110
+  10111011
```
01 carry 1

Now we go to the next digit to the left. There is a 1 and a 0. This adds up to 1, plus our 1 carry, again giving us 10, so we write in the 0 and carry 1.

```
  110010110
+  10111011
```
001 carry 1

Again we add 0 and 1 to get 1, plus our 1 carry giving us 10, so we write in the zero and carry 1.

```
  110010110
+  10111011
```
0001 carry 1

Now we have an even more complicated problem. What is 1 + 1 + 1 in binary arithmetic? Well, let's break it down. We know 1 + 1 = 10. What is 10 + 1? Well, that is easy, 10 + 1 = 11. So this time we write in the 1 and carry 1.

```
  110010110
+  10111011
```
10001 carry 1

The next step is similar to the others we have done before.

```
  110010110
+  10111011
```
010001 carry 1

Finally we reach a place where we don't carry.

```
  110010110
+  10111011
```
1010001

The last two digits both carry so the answer requires one more digit than we have had so far.

```
  110010110
+  10111011
───────────
 1001010001
```

If you like you can check this out in base-ten arithmetic. The first binary number (110010110) is equivalent to 406 in base-ten. The second number (10111011) is 187. The total (1001010001) is 593. Check.

You note a number of things when you actually go through this process. First, you learn how to add small binary numbers.

$$0 + 0 = 0$$
$$0 + 1 = 1$$
$$1 + 0 = 1$$
$$1 + 1 = 10$$
$$1 + 1 + 1 = 11$$

Second, the binary system requires an awful lot of carrying. Well, that's to be expected. Given how quickly it runs out of numbers, we keep having to shift up one digit.

SUBTRACTION

Let's try subtraction; only this time we will prepare beforehand by looking at some equations.

$$0 - 0 = 0$$
$$1 - 0 = 1$$
$$1 - 1 = 0$$

But how do we solve the following problem?

$$0 - 1 = ?$$

In base-ten arithmetic, when the simple subtraction would produce a negative number we add 10 to the digit in the minuend (the minuend is the number from which we are subtracting the subtrahend), subtract and then add 10 to the digit in the subtrahend. This addition of 10 to minuend and subtrahend is called "borrowing." Here is an example:

minuend   43
subtrahend   − 24
                 ——————
                 9 borrow 1

We pretend the 3 in the minuend is a 13 and subtract the first digit of the subtrahend (3 − 4 = 13 − 4 borrow 1 = 9 borrow 1). That means we must return the borrowed 1 to the next digit. The next subtraction is then 4 − 3 instead of 4 − 2:

$$\begin{array}{r} 43 \\ -\,24 \\ \hline 19 \end{array}$$

In each case of borrowing, then, we must always remember to replace the borrowed 1 by adding it to the next digit in the subtrahend. The same principle applies to base-two problems.

In multi-digited base-two arithmetic the problem can be restated as follows:

$0 - 1 = 10 - 1$ borrow $1 = 1$ borrow 1

Two other situations should be looked at before we do an actual problem.

$0 - 10 = 10 - 10$ borrow $1 = 0$ borrow 1

$1 - 10 = 11 - 10$ borrow $1 = 1$ borrow 1

With these three examples behind us let's try a real problem. The first step is easy:

$$\begin{array}{r} 1001010001 \\ -\ \ 110010110 \\ \hline 1 \end{array}$$

But with the second digit we must use the borrowing procedure.

$$
\begin{array}{r}
1001010001 \\
- 110010110 \\
\hline
\end{array}
$$
11 borrow 1

We have to add the borrowed 1 to the next digit in the subtrahend, a 1. That operation then becomes $0 - 10 = 0$ borrow 1.

$$
\begin{array}{r}
1001010001 \\
- 110010110 \\
\hline
\end{array}
$$
011 borrow 1

Here we have a $0 - 1$ situation, so we write the 1 and borrow 1.

$$
\begin{array}{r}
1001010001 \\
- 110010110 \\
\hline
\end{array}
$$
1011 borrow 1

Now we have a $1 - 10$ situation. This leaves 1 and we borrow 1.

$$
\begin{array}{r}
1001010001 \\
- 110010110 \\
\hline
\end{array}
$$
11011 borrow 1

Now we have a $0 - 1$ situation. Write the 1 and borrow 1.

$$
\begin{array}{r}
1001010001 \\
- 110010110 \\
\hline
\end{array}
$$
111011 borrow 1

At last we have a place with no borrowing! The carry leaves a $1 - 1 = 0$.

```
  1001010001
-  110010110
-------------
   0111011
```

The next step requires a borrow.

```
  1001010001
-  110010110
-------------
  10111011 borrow 1
```

The next step is $0 - 10 = 0$ borrow 1 and the last step is $1 - 1 = 0$.

```
  1001010001
-  110010110
-------------
  0010111011
```

and we are all through.

At this point you should note that this is the same as the addition problem only this time it is worked in reverse.

There is another way to do subtraction. Suppose you want to subtract a subtrahend represented by Y from a minuend represented by Z. You first find something called the binary complement of Y. The complement is a number in which all the 1s are changed to 0s and all the 0s to 1s. Then 1 is added. For example, 1010101 becomes $0101010 + 1 = 101011$. Or 11011 becomes $00100 + 1 = 101$. Then you add the binary complement to Z. Let's try it with the subtraction problem we just did. The complement of Y, which was 110010110, is $001101001 + 1 = 1101010$. (Note that we drop the 0s when they fall in the most significant digit place just as we do in base-ten arithmetic. We would not write 00100 when we mean 100.)

Having found the complement of Y we now simply add it to Z:

```
    1001010001
  +    1101010
  _____
    1010111011
```

and then you drop the *most* significant digit (plus the 0 which now occupies the most significant place) leaving 10111011.

To repeat, in this method of subtraction you first find the binary complement (change all the 1s to 0s and all the 0s to 1s and add 1) of the subtrahend, then add it to the minuend, then drop the most significant digit of the sum and you have the difference. All these operations are simple for the computer to perform as we will see.

MULTIPLICATION

Multiplication with binary numbers is a delight because you are multiplying with only 0 or 1. Remember long multiplication? Starting with the least significant digit of the multiplier, you step across the multiplicand digit by digit, carrying where necessary.

```
    326
  × 105
  _____
    0 carry 3
```

The result of the first multiplication is 30, so you write 0 and carry 3. Next is $5 \times 2 = 10$ plus the 3 carry $= 13$. Write the 3 and carry 1.

```
    326
  × 105
  _____
    30 carry 1
```

The last product of this digit is 15, and since there is no further multiplication on this line you add the 1 being carried and write it all in. This completes the first digit and its row.

$$\begin{array}{r} 326 \\ \times\,105 \\ \hline 1630 \end{array}$$

Now we go on to the second digit in the multiplier. Its row looks like this.

$$\begin{array}{r} 326 \\ \times\,105 \\ \hline 1630 \\ 0 \end{array}$$

Remember, we had to move over one place for the second multiplier. The third multiplying digit looks like this.

$$\begin{array}{r} 326 \\ \times\,105 \\ \hline 1630 \\ 0 \\ 326 \end{array}$$

Now we add.

$$\begin{array}{r} 326 \\ \times\,105 \\ \hline 1630 \\ 0 \\ 326 \\ \hline 34230 \end{array}$$

Rather a tedious process, but it works. The example at the top of page 31 shows how the same problem would be done in binary form.

```
              101000110
     ×         1101001
              101000110
                      0
                     0
           101000110
                  0
        101000110
       101000110
       ─────────────────
     1000010110110110
```

If the digit you are multiplying by is a 0 you just step over one place. If it is a 1 you copy the multiplicand. By adding the results you have the product. Multiplication in binary arithmetic is therefore simply a matter of stepping over and copying the multiplicand as often as called for by the 1s in the multiplier and then adding.

DIVISION

The most difficult of the four arithmetical functions—both for people and for computers—is division. A computer can do it the way we do, but long division is not a favorite chore for anyone. A somewhat simpler technique which computers do well because they function so fast with addition or subtraction is a sequence of repetitive subtractions or additions.

Suppose you wish to divide number Z by number Y. The computer adds Y to itself over and over, checking after each addition to see if the new sum is larger than Z. When the sum is larger than Z the number of times it ran the sequence is one more than the desired result. When the sum is the same as Z the number of times it ran the sequence is exactly equal to the desired result. For example, suppose the computer is dividing 11110 by 110. It starts by adding 110 to itself and keeps a running count plus a running sum.

$$\begin{array}{r} 110 \\ + 110 \\ \hline 1100 \\ + 110 \\ \hline 10010 \\ + 110 \\ \hline 11000 \\ + 110 \\ \hline 11110 \end{array}$$ count 1
count 10 (2)

count 11 (3)

count 100 (4)

count 101 (5)

An exact match!

So the division of 11110 (= 30) by 110 (= 6) is 101 (= 5).

Division can also be done by subtracting the divisor (Y) from the dividend (Z) as often as is necessary to bring Z down to zero. This is the literal interpretation of dividing—how many times does the divisor go into the dividend? A computer subtracts it as often as necessary, and when it has reduced the dividend to zero reports the count.

As you can see, division requires a lot of different functions—a succession of additions or subtractions, a repetitive comparison of the remainder with zero, and a continuing count of the number of operations being performed. Furthermore, if the division is to be performed with considerable accuracy—to many decimal places—then it may be necessary to shift the divisor over one place to the right when a small remainder is still to be accounted for and the entire subtraction sequence repeated. This is why division can take 20 to 50 times as long as addition or subtraction. This is also why computer programmers talk of elegant or efficient "algorithms" when they do their jobs. An algorithm is a method of calculating something—a method of performing division, for example—and as we saw there are at least two and actually several dozen ways to do the job. The least costly in time and effort is the most elegant in the eyes of the programmer. It will save time and memory and allow him to do more elaborate programs faster and easier.

BASE-SIXTEEN ARITHMETIC

When humans must talk to computers directly in binary numbers, the long strings of 1s and 0s are easy to misread and miswrite, so a compromise system is used. Two hexadecimal (base-sixteen) digits neatly represent eight bits of a binary number:

Binary	Hex
00000000	00
00000001	01
00000010	02
00000011	03
00000100	04
00000101	05
00000110	06
00000111	07
00001000	08
00001001	09
00001010	0A
00001011	0B
00001100	0C
00001101	0D
00001110	0E
00001111	0F
00010000	10
00010001	11
00010010	12
00010011	13

Eight binary digits will count from 0 to 255 (decimal) and from 00 to FF in hexadecimal notation. When you see a strange set of numbers and letters in a computer instruction book, say 40B3H, the last "H" is the tipoff that it is a hexadecimal number—I leave it to you to figure out what 40B3 is.

DECIMAL POINTS

For decimal points we have to review what a point is in base-ten arithmetic. A number like 123.45 means 123 plus $\frac{4}{10}$ plus $\frac{5}{100}$. Each step to the right of the decimal point divides by the base (10) just as each step to the left of the decimal point multiplies by 10. Exactly the same principle holds for binary arithmetic. A number like 1110.101 is (in base-ten) 14 plus $\frac{1}{2}$ plus $\frac{1}{4}$ plus $\frac{1}{8}$. And just as 9.99999 is almost 10, so 11.11111 is almost 4. It is 3 plus $\frac{1}{2}$ plus $\frac{1}{4}$ plus $\frac{1}{8}$ plus $\frac{1}{16}$ plus $\frac{1}{32}$. In base-ten terms it is $3\frac{31}{32}$.

LOGIC

Almost a hundred years before the first electronic computer was built, an English mathematician named George Boole invented a mathematics of logic that has guided the structure of every electronic computer now working. Boolean algebra, as it is called, applies a formal set of rules to logical statements. As a result, elaborate statements can be examined and their truth proved or disproved in exactly the same way that a theorem is proved or disproved in geometry using the rules of ordinary algebra.

Logic is not concerned with numbers but with statements that are either true or false. We assign the value 1 to a true statement and 0 to a false one. Boolean algebra starts with three basic operations—NOT, AND, and OR. Each of these functions in a computer circuit is called an "operator." As you might suspect, the NOT operation simply takes a 1 and changes it to a 0 or takes a 0 and changes it to a 1. To show these changes we use something called a truth table:

A	not-A
0	1
1	0

You read this as follows: When A is 0, not-A is 1. When A is 1, not-A is 0.

To help visualize complex operations, computer people use diagrams representing the electronic circuitry which will perform these operations. The diagram for this operation is:

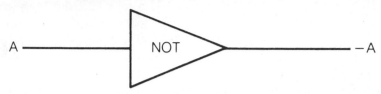

When a signal meaning 1 comes in on the line from the left, the electric circuit in the NOT box switches it to its opposite (represented by a -A). There is an obvious application of this operation for the circuit in subtraction when we need to find the binary complement of a number.

The AND operation has a special meaning for the word "and." When the two inputs to the AND operation are both 1 the output is 1. If either of the inputs is 0 the output is 0. The symbol for the AND is an asterisk (*). Here is the truth table for the AND operation.

A	B	A*B
0	0	0
0	1	0
1	0	0
1	1	1

2041307

Note that if you want to include many inputs to the AND operation, the expression is similar and the operation is the same. Thus A*B*C*D will output a 1 only if all four inputs are 1s. Otherwise the output is 0.

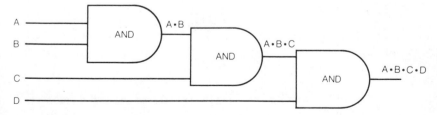

The last basic Boolean operation is OR. This also produces a single output from two inputs, but now the output is a 1 when either one of the inputs is a 1. The symbol for this operation is a plus sign (+).

A	B	A+B
0	0	0
0	1	1
1	0	1
1	1	1

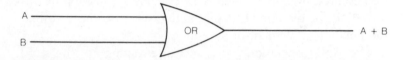

Boolean algebra is different from arithmetic in that there are only two values—1 and 0—but the entire binary system and all its arithmetic can be made out of these three operations. For example, suppose you were doing an addition of two binary numbers. The numbers might be large enough to require a dozen or more binary digits. However, let's just consider the first digit for the moment. We can write a truth table for the addition which would look like this:

A	B	SUM
0	0	0
0	1	1
1	0	1
1	1	0 carry 1

This is not exactly like either Boolean operation AND or OR, but it has similarities. You can put together a diagram made up of Boolean operations that produces a truth table just like it.

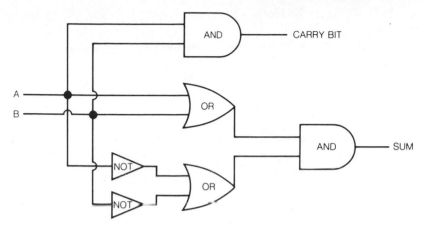

Here, when A and B are 0 the sum is 0 and the carry is 0. When either A or B is 1 and the other is 0 the sum is 1 and the carry is 0. When A and B are both 1 the sum is 0 and the carry is 1. The carry would then be added in a circuit with the next larger digit while the sum would be saved as the proper answer for this digit.

STORAGE

One further circuit that can be made up of the Boolean operations is called a latching circuit or a flip-flop. The idea is that when a bit is signaled to be a 1, somehow the system should recognize it as such and remember, even though the signal may have stopped. Similarly, if a bit is signaled to be a 0, the circuit should now switch to 0 and keep that until informed otherwise.

Here is a combination of Boolean elements which does exactly that. The circuit will not react unless the "control" input is a 1. This is because the circuit would have no other way of knowing when it was getting a 0 as a signal rather than the system just being at rest.

| | Data | |
Control	Input	Output
0	0	No Change
0	1	No Change
1	0	0
1	1	1

When the control signal is a 1 and the data input is a 1 the output is a 1. If the control signal goes to 0 the output remains a 1, held there by a feedback going to the upper pair. If the control signal is a 1 and the data input is a 0, the output switches to 0 and will stay a 0 until both control signal and data input go to 1.

The significance of this exercise is that with simple electronic circuits that do the Boolean operations we can build a machine that will count, add, subtract, multiply, divide, and remember in binary arithmetic. In short, we have an electronic computer.

3

THE THINKING PLACE

By the mid-forties the stage was set and the curtain ready to go up. Babbage had given us the ideas, Boole the logical algebra, and in response to wartime needs the first crude machines were built. However, it was clear that unless something dramatic happened, digital computers would be of use only to large institutions like the federal government or billion-dollar business corporations. No one foresaw the possibility that they might eventually become a home appliance until the technological breakthrough that was to change so much of our world.

TRANSISTORS

In 1948 three Bell Laboratories scientists, John Bardeen, Walter H. Brattain, and William B. Shockley, demonstrated the first transistor and, unlike many truly revolutionary developments, this one was recognized at once. The transistor was the first in a new field of "solid-state electronics," so-called because the electrons are moved and controlled through a solid crystalline material rather than in the evacuated spaces of a vacuum tube. The small size, the elimination of the hot filament, and the lower cost led manufacturers to jump at the device. Within 24 months transistors were being sold in small radios at prices often less than half of their vacuum tube counterparts. They were so popular that the word "transistor" came to mean the portable, battery-operated radio rather than the tiny device inside.

Soon, transistors of higher power-handling capacity were appearing in high-fidelity equipment, television sets, and, of course, in the new computers. More than any other technological achievement, the invention of the transistor took mankind well beyond the Industrial Revolution.

Without the transistor the computer as we know it today is an impossibility. As we saw earlier, mechanical counters driven by gears are impractical because they are slow, need a lot of power to get into motion and to stop, wear out after a few million counts, and are bulky. Vacuum tubes offer speed, but also take a lot of electrical power to get the filament hot enough to boil off clouds of electrons, and the heat generated is so great that large air-conditioning systems are necessary to keep the computers cool. Also, the limited lifetime of the filaments means that tubes will burn out and the computer will go "down" every day or two, and the mere size of the tubes, when multiplied by the thousands, adds up to a monstrous machine. With the development of transistors it became possible to build full capability computers the size of an office desk or smaller.

What is this miraculous device, the transistor? Its essential ingredient is a bit of crystalline material called a semiconductor. As this term implies, the semiconductor can conduct electricity less effectively than the conductive metals but better than plastics, glass, or rubber. Usually the latter materials are so nonconductive that they are used as insulators. Most transistors are made of silicon or germanium as the base material which has been mixed (a process called "doping" for some reason) with impurity elements in tiny zones on its surface.

A single transistor has three wires connected to it. Each is in contact with a different zone. A source of direct current, such as a battery, is connected across the two outer wires. Electricity from the power source tries to flow through the semiconductor but it is stopped by the poor conductivity of the material. When the third wire (sometimes called the "gate") has a positive voltage applied to it, the semiconductor changes state. It becomes a good conductor with the current flowing freely in the same way that the opening of a faucet permits water to flow freely.

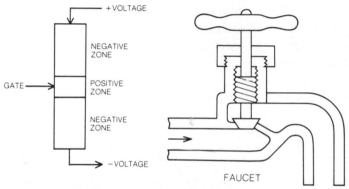

It takes very little effort, very little electric power at the gate, to turn the transistor "on" or "off," but a small change in the control voltage can produce a large change in the output current. This effect is called power amplification. Without amplification the signals that are going through a computer would slowly weaken and eventually become too tiny to work even as a gate. We have the same effect in long telephone lines. The telephone company has to install amplifiers every few miles so that the electric signals that represent your voice will be strong enough to activate the speaker in the receiver at the other end. In our computer, electric voltages representing binary digits will be moved from circuit to circuit, doing arithmetic, storing, printing, displaying numbers and letters on screens, and we don't want them to fade in the process.

A second important characteristic of the transistor is that it can be made very small. The first transistor was a few hundredths of an inch long. Transistors can now be made in a few millionths of an inch of semiconductor material. We can expect within one more generation of Large Scale Integrated Circuits (which combine thousands of transistors on the surface of one "chip" of silicon or germanium) that transistors may approach the size of the crystal molecules themselves.

Here is just one transistor a few thousandths of an inch long in a cross section of a large integrated circuit that can contain thousands. Metal conductors are connected to the zones through holes in an insulating coating on the surface of the crystal. Most of the interconnections between transistors are made in a metallic second layer deposited on the surface of the insulating layer which is then selectively etched away to leave a "printed circuit." Thus thousands of transistors make a complex electric device on one semiconductor chip.

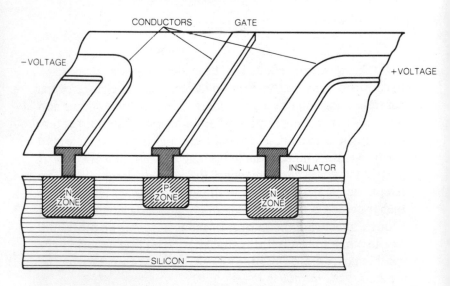

Transistors offer everything necessary to construct a computer. They are tiny, waste little power, and amplify. The production process is critical—doping, etching for the connectors, soldering of connectors—all these procedures require super-clean rooms and fairly advanced chemistry. But once it is made and sealed in its case, a transistor will last indefinitely. There is nothing to wear out and nothing to overheat unless too much current is pushed through.

A transistor or two can be easily hooked up to function like a Boolean operator. For example, consider the NOT function.

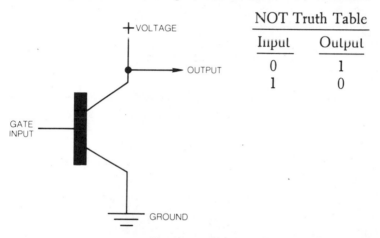

NOT Truth Table

Input	Output
0	1
1	0

In this diagram the transistor is represented by the short, heavy vertical line with three thinner lines, representing the three wires, extending up, down, and to the left. A direct-current source is applied at the top wire, and the current would like to go down through the transistor and out the bottom wire (here drawn with the engineer's "ground" symbol). The semiconductor material will not permit current to flow as long as the input gate is at zero voltage. Since the current is blocked, it tries to squirt out through the output wire. Thus, when the input is zero the output is high. We arbitrarily call a high voltage a binary 1 and a low or zero voltage a binary 0, so when the input is 0 the output is 1.

When the input is high the transistor conducts. All the current goes rushing down through the semiconductor material which now offers an easier path. Therefore the output goes to 0. To repeat, when the input is 0 the output is 1. When the input is 1 the output is 0—a perfect NOT function for our computer.

We don't have to work our way through the AND and OR circuits. Engineers have designed hundreds of complex and ingenious circuits for these and for many other much more complicated functions. Other components like resistors and capacitors sometimes have to be used along with the transistors to make the circuits work properly. These components are combined in many different ways to make it possible to add, subtract, multiply, divide, count, compare two numbers, and store numbers.

Each desired function can be described by a truth table of 1s and 0s, and once you have a truth table it is relatively easy to design a circuit that will do the job. It may require 25 transistors to add two bits together and, as we saw, binary numbers need a lot of bits to make up a large number. It takes about 500 transistors to add two 16-bit numbers. But if we can put a million transistors on a semiconductor "chip," which is a quarter inch on a side, we won't have to worry too much about using 500 of them to add a couple of numbers.

THE CENTRAL PROCESSING UNIT

In a computer arithmetical calculations actually take place on a chip called the central processing unit. In early computers the central processing chip handled arithmetic and nothing more. However, as manufacturers were able to add more and more transistors to the same chip, many other functions were incorporated at a saving in space and cost.

The most important section of the central processing unit is still the arithmetic and logic unit. Here are the circuits that will accept a bit, add it to another, carry 1 if necessary, and add the carry to the next digit. There are circuits that automatically find the binary complement of a number so that subtractions can be done quickly by adding the complement. Adding circuits are used to do multiplication and division, but comparisons are done by another set of circuits.

Closely associated with the arithmetic unit is a special transistor circuit called the "accumulator." The accumulator is a short-term memory made from a flip-flop or latching circuit. The computer stores a number in the accumulator, adds numbers to the number stored there, subtracts numbers from what is there, and compares other numbers to it. There are also other memory banks like the accumulator. These others are usually called "registers." The more registers in the central processing unit the more powerful it is, since computing is faster and more efficient when there are lots of places to put numbers, at least temporarily. Note that the accumulator and these other registers are not intended to keep numbers for any length of time. They act as the computer's scratch pad where numbers are stored while they are being worked on.

Finally, the central processing unit has a control unit which directs the flow of data and instructions from register to register and to the arithmetic unit. The control unit is the traffic manager and the switchboard of the computer. The control unit receives orders from outside the central processing unit and directs the operations inside accordingly. It is the controller that tells the arithmetic unit whether to add, subtract, multiply, or divide. It directs the flow of numbers in and around the central processing unit and delivers the results outside.

One other important circuit should be mentioned here because it is so much a part of what goes on in the central processing unit even though it is usually a separate circuit in the computer. This is the computer "clock." The bigger and newer central processing units have the clock built right in with the controller and arithmetic units. Others are on a separate chip nearby. Whether it is on the same chip or not, the clock sends out a regular electric pulse like a drumbeat going on in the background continuously. These pulses are used to time all the operations of the computer.

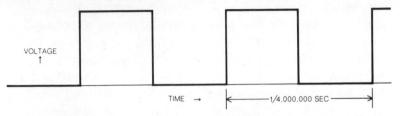

Here is the way the pulses look. For one small instant the voltage is high (a binary 1 according to our convention); for the next instant the voltage is low (a binary 0). These pulses go to all parts of the computer as long as the computer is running. For most home computers the clock pulses are at a frequency of two million beats per second and the newer central processing units now operate at four million beats per second. This means it is one four-millionth of a second between the start of one beat and the start of the next.

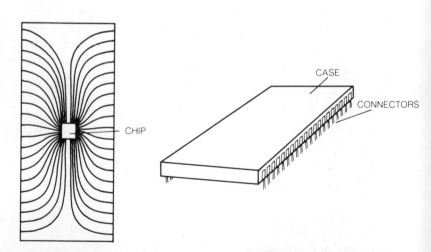

The preceding drawings illustrate a central processing unit chip and how it is encased. The chip with all the circuits we have described measures only a $\frac{1}{4}$ inch on each side. Forty wires connect to the chip to bring in and take out information. The chip plus connecting wires are sealed in a plastic case that measures approximately $\frac{5}{8}$ inch wide, 2 inches long, and $\frac{1}{16}$ inch thick. The case size is actually dictated by the number of connectors that have to be brought into the chip.

HOW BIG A BYTE?

We have to take a small detour here to understand the kinds of signals that come into and go out through those 40 connectors. As we know, each bit requires a separate circuit to store, add, or otherwise operate on it. Engineers had to decide how many bits would normally be worked on as one number in order to know how many circuits to provide.

Microcomputers normally work with eight bits as a good compromise between size and efficiency. Eight bits will provide 256 unique numbers and this is adequate for most purposes. They call this eight-bit number a "byte," and as we track binary numbers around the computer we will be using the word very often. While 256 unique numbers may not seem very large, one must remember that it is always possible to make a larger number out of two or perhaps even three bytes. A two-byte number has 65,536 unique bit patterns, a three-byte number has 16,777,216 patterns. If the numbers are large enough to require two bytes, the first byte represents the eight least significant bits, the second byte represents the eight most significant bits. For addition, the arithmetic unit works on the least significant byte first, does the sum, stores the result, and sets aside the carry. Then it works on the most significant byte plus the carry and stores the result somewhere else. This procedure takes more time than if the computer worked on the entire number at once, but since such large numbers are used only rarely it is much more economical to use eight-bit numbers.

We keep referring to the bytes as numbers, but the computer really doesn't care whether the string of eight bits is a number, a Greek letter, or a mathematical symbol. The symbol can be anything one chooses. The computer is perfectly willing to store, compare, and do logic functions on any byte no matter what it represents.

With so many unique bit patterns in an eight-bit byte, we can assign a different pattern to each uppercase and lowercase alphabetical letter, the arabic numerals 0 to 9, punctuation marks, and all other symbols normally used in writing and still have enough bits left over for special purposes. Of course, if the arithmetic unit thinks it is adding the bit code for the letter X to the bit code for the letter Y, it would produce a nonsensical bit code as the total. The instructions have to be appropriate. If one asks for absurd operations on what the computer simply knows as "data," absurd answers result. This is a problem we will deal with later.

Bit codes for the alphabet have been standardized among most manufacturers of computers so that their equipment can be hooked up to communicate with each other. In fact only seven bits are needed for the identification, which provides 128 different combinations. The eighth bit is used as a special checking signal so that when different computers talk to each other they can be sure no errors have been introduced by the transmission lines connecting them. This set of bit patterns is standardized as "ASCII" codes, which stands for American Standard Code for Information Interchange and is pronounced "askey." Here are a few of the codes:

1000001	A	1100001	a
1000010	B	1100010	b
1000011	C	1100011	c
1000100	D	1100100	d

1000101	E	1100101	e
1000110	F	1100110	f
1000111	G	1100111	g
1001000	H	1101000	h
1001001	I	1101001	i
1001010	J	1101010	j
1001011	K	1101011	k
1001100	L	1101100	l
1001101	M	1101101	m
1001110	N	1101110	n
1001111	O	1101111	o
1010000	P	1110000	p
1010001	Q	1110001	q
1010010	R	1110010	r
1010011	S	1110011	s
1010100	T	1110100	t
1010101	U	1110101	u
1010110	V	1110110	v
1010111	W	1110111	w
1011000	X	1111000	x
1011001	Y	1111001	y
1011010	Z	1111010	z
1011011	[	1111011	{
1011100	\	1111100	|
1011101	]	1111101	}
1011110	^	1111110	~
1011111	—	1111111	delete
0100000	space	0110000	0
0100001	!	0110001	1
0100010	"	0110010	2
0100011	#	0110011	3
0100100	$	0110100	4
0100101	%	0110101	5
0100110	&	0110110	6
0100111	´	0110111	7

0101000	(	0111000	8
0101001	)	0111001	9
0101010	*	0111010	:
0101011	+	0111011	;
0101100	,	0111100	<
0101101	-	0111101	=
0101110	.	0111110	>
0101111	/	0111111	?

Now if you want to write a letter to someone you can type in the words, letter by letter in these codes, and instruct the computer to store them in proper order. Then when you are ready to have it typed back, or when the person to whom it is written wants to read it, it can be recalled from memory and "played" back on a screen.

PARALLEL OR SERIAL?

One other decision had to be made about how numbers were to be handled inside a computer before the engineers could actually get started on the design. This decision was whether the arithmetic and other functions were to be done on a byte, one bit at a time, or whether they would be done on all the bits at once. When we add two numbers longhand we work on the digits from right to left, one at a time. But the computer works so fast that it can easily handle all the bits and their carries in the same time interval. That makes the whole operation so much faster and more powerful that the engineers didn't really have to think about this for long. If the mathematical operations are done serially, it will take eight times longer to examine and work on each byte than if they are all done at the same time. We can't afford to use that much time for each operation, so the decision was to do it all at once—but there is a fairly heavy cost in hardware and there are some other problems as well.

In order to handle all eight bits at the same time each has to travel through its own connecting wire to the central processing unit and once within this unit to the arithmetic unit and the various registers. For larger numbers we'll need two bytes, which means we have 16 connecting wires going everywhere in the computer just to carry the data bytes around. Another 16 wires carry address codes. This group of 16 or 32 wires is part of a larger bundle of wires called a "bus." The bus in many home computers may contain as many as 100 wires. Not all wires are used at the same time and many are not used at all, but most computers do need fifty or more in the normal course of operation. As special accessories are added, the spare wires are pressed into service.

The signals carried by the bus are in the form of direct-current voltages—high for a 1, negative or low for a 0 bit. The voltage may change abruptly at the end of each clock cycle, so if you were monitoring the voltage of the data bus over a number of clock cycles it might look like this. Under each cycle you'll find the byte code in 0s and 1s.

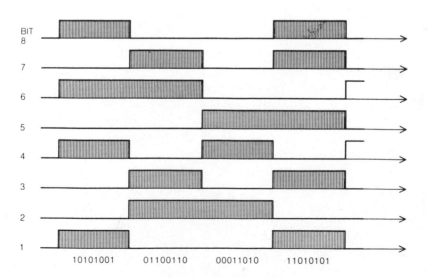

BIT
8

7

6

5

4

3

2

1

10101001   01100110   00011010   11010101

REVIEW

Let's review what we have in hardware related to the central processing unit before going on to the actual operation.

—We have an arithmetic and logic unit capable of doing arithmetic functions, comparisons, and simple logic like the AND, NOT, and OR operations.

—We have an accumulator closely associated with the arithmetic unit to provide temporary memory storage for numbers being worked on in the arithmetic unit.

—We have several other registers for the temporary storage of bytes.

—We have a controller which generally oversees what is connected to what and when.

—We have a clock which beats out regular cycles to all parts of the computer.

—We have a bundle of wires connecting the various parts of the central processing unit to each other, to the controller, to the registers, to the clock, and to other outside components of the computer. This is called a bus.

Here is a typical arrangement of these elements in the central processing unit.

REGISTERS	ARITHMETIC + LOGIC UNIT	
CLOCK	CONTROL UNIT	
	DATA BUS	

THE MESSAGES

We now know something about the central processing unit hardware—the wires, transistors, and other components built into and around the central processing unit. Let's see what information actually goes through these circuits and how it is organized and decoded.

In addition to the clock pulses going around the computer there are three distinct kinds of information to be dealt with. The first is data—binary numbers or the codes listed above for the alphabetical characters and other symbols of human language. We also need instructions which will tell the computer at each step what it is to do next. Finally we need something that works like a filing system. The data and instructions will be stored in the registers and other memory locations in the computer, so some means of finding and retrieving them when needed has to be figured out. The method used is to assign a different "address" to every memory location in the computer.

Most addresses will have to be two bytes long, giving us 65,536 different addresses if needed.

The addresses and the instructions are in the same eight-bit bytes used for data or alphabetical symbols, so some way has to be used to warn the computer when the byte is data, when it is instruction, and when an address. This is where the clock pulses come in. The clock beats out a four-quarter time. During the first quarter the computer looks at a "program counter"—a register which starts counting at 0 when the computer is turned on and increases one number each cycle until something tells it to stop. This counter therefore always knows precisely where the computer is in its progress through a job.

When the computer is in the first quarter of the cycle it looks at the contents of the program counter, which directs it to a memory address where an instruction is stored. During the second quarter the contents of that memory location are transferred to a special register used only to store instructions. During the third quarter the program counter is checked again (it has moved up one count) for the memory address of a byte of data. During the fourth quarter the instruction is carried out.

Note the instruction may simply be to move the data from one place to another, it may be to perform an arithmetical function, it may be to wait while something else in the computer is going on, or it may be to open a line to the display screen. Not all instructions necessarily work on data. Some set the computer for a different mode of operation.

Here are the six cycles required to direct the computer through an addition:

1.1 Program counter connected to bus. It reads 0.

1.2 Memory location 0 connected through bus to instruction register. It finds a code instructing the controller to transfer the contents of the next address to general register 1.

1.3 Program counter connected to bus. It reads 1.

1.4 Memory location 1 connected through bus to general register 1.

2.1 Program counter connected to bus. It reads 10.

2.2 Memory location 10 connected through bus to instruction register. It finds a code to transfer the contents of the next address to the accumulator.

2.3 Program counter connected to bus. It reads 11.

2.4 Memory location 11 connected through bus to accumulator.

3.1 Program counter connected to bus. It reads 100.

3.2 Memory location 100 connected through bus to instruction register. It finds a code to add the contents of general register 1 to the contents of the accumulator.

3.3 Idle. No need to read the contents of the program counter in this cycle.

3.4 Contents of register 1 added to accumulator.

4.1 Program counter connected to bus. It reads 101.

4.2 Memory location 101 connected through bus to instruction register. It finds a code to store the contents of the next address in general register 2.

4.3 Program counter connected to bus. It reads 110.

4.4 Memory location 110 connected through bus to register 2. It stores its address there.

5.1 Program counter connected to bus. It reads 111.

5.2 Memory location 111 connected through bus to instruction register. It has the code to transfer the contents of the accumulator to the address in register 2.

5.3 Program counter connected to bus. It reads 1000.

5.4 Accumulator connected to address given in register 2.

6.1 Program counter connected to bus. It reads 1001.

6.2 Memory location 1001 connected through the bus to instruction register. It reads code to stop.

6.3 All operations stop.

Tedious? You bet! But the computer doesn't get bored, and in any case the total time to run through these 23 instructions would be about one hundred-thousandth of a second. At that speed there is no possibility that the human operator could feed the instructions to the computer by hand. Instead, as we have seen, the instruction list is placed in a rising sequence of memory locations beforehand so that when it needs the next order the computer will readily find it.

As you look at this list you will see that half the steps are just checking back with the program counter for the location of the next instruction and the transfer of that instruction to the instruction register. As for the instructions themselves, almost all are concerned with moving numbers from one specified location to another—either a register in the central processing unit, the accumulator, or a memory location identified by an address outside the central processing unit.

The instructions are byte codes like all the other numbers. How does the central processing unit know what to do? Well, the controller has built into its hardware the ability to receive, recognize, and act on a whole list of coded instructions. When it finds one of these codes in the instruction register it automatically connects the called-for registers to the bus and hooks up the proper circuits in the arithmetic unit if they are required. Most central processing units can recognize around a hundred such basic instructions. The newest central processing units can recognize 158. Most of them have to do with moving bytes from one location to another, and only a very few actually change a byte or call for a mathematical function. The codes that signal these instructions are called "machine language."

It is possible to talk to the computer directly in machine language one cycle at a time—though that means the machine is waiting for your next instruction an interminable number of cycles. It is also possible to write the list of instructions one by one into memory. Some hobbyists like to do this the hard way. They know all 158 instruction codes, and they enter them in the memory by hand. It takes a long time, but they know precisely how the numbers or letters will move around through the computer at every step of its operation.

An easier way is to let the computer write the program for you, because it is tedious work, follows straightforward rules, and involves a lot of detail. We'll be spending some time on the subject of programming later because it is the only way we can instruct the computer to do what we wish. But don't worry; there are much simpler languages—simpler for humans, that is—available.

4

MEMORIES

The accumulator and other registers in the central processing unit work as the blackboard memory of the computer. They are convenient for storing bytes, but they can hold only one byte in each register. We need room for hundreds and often thousands of bytes for programs, data, text of letters, and so on. Storage of this amount is provided in other memory banks in the computer as well as in more permanent "archival" storage units outside the computer, in what are called "peripheral" devices.

Let's be sure about precisely what it is we are storing. Instructions, data, or addresses are coded in eight-bit bytes. Most of the time more than one byte is necessary for an address or for data. The address and the data are sent one after the other during two different clock cycles. Each bit is either a positive d.c. voltage or a zero voltage on each of the eight conductors of the bus.

We need to be able to store the data in a memory place identified by an address so that later, when the central processing unit reconnects to that address, the stored byte will again appear on the bus.

Technical development in computer memory has been so rapid and it has gone in so many different directions that we now have a bewildering choice of devices, each with advantages and disadvantages in cost, speed, permanence, and ease of use. Ideally, we would like very large capacity in very small space, always immediately accessible to the computer, and as permanent or temporary as the particular application may require. We would also like this at a very low cost.

There is no such memory available now but something similar can be expected soon. The size and cost of present-day memories are only one-thousandth of what they were ten years ago, and another substantial reduction is expected over the next decade.

There is a lot of jargon in the computer business and I have tried to be very careful about not using it. For example, a central processing unit is called a CPU; an arithmetic and logic unit is an ALU. A bus, thank goodness, is just a bus. But when it comes to memories they get out of hand. I'll give you the jargon or the abbreviation so that you can recognize them, but I plan to spell out the words each time at the risk of having to type and typeset a few more bytes. For starters, when you store a byte of data you "write" it, when you retrieve it you "read" it. These are exactly analogous to the process of recording and playing back on a tape recorder.

The most important division of memories is between those that actually reside in the computer in electronic form (as in the transistor circuits we looked at earlier) and those that are peripheral or outside the main computer frame. Inside it is the all-electronic memory; outside memories are almost all moving magnetic surface devices which are very similar to tape recorders in their principles of operation. The two kinds of memory also differ in another important way. The all-electronic memory usually provides access to any address directly: that is, if you want the data in memory cell number 2,468 (to resort to base-ten numbers for the moment), the computer can reach out to that address directly and read the data located there. This is called random-access memory (jargon: RAM) because the address is selectable at random among all the other addresses.

By contrast, moving magnetic surface memories require that you search through some section of the magnetic medium until you get to the place where the desired data are stored. The distance traveled may be as long as 60 minutes of tape or as short as one circle on a magnetized disk rotating at 3,600 revolutions per minute. But any moving surface memory gets us back to mechanical motions which take much more time than electron movements in circuits. Engineers would concentrate on all-electronic memory except for two things—cost and permanence. Most electronic memories disappear when you turn the power switch off, so the bread-and-butter letter to your aunt would be gone when you came to find it the next day. Magnetic moving surface memories are, for all practical purposes, permanent. You can put the tape cassette on a shelf for a year and then take it down and play it back (read it) without dropping a bit.

With these general principles in mind we can take a look at each type, see how it works, what the good points and problems are, and then go on to see what changes are likely to occur in the next few years.

CORE

In the 1950s and 1960s electronic memories were called "core" after the doughnut-shaped ring of magnetic material which is used to store each bit. The cores are about the size of a pinhead, and they are strung together in rectangular arrays like a coarsely woven cloth.

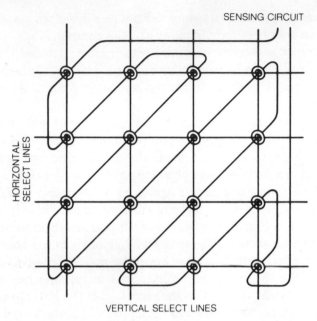

SENSING CIRCUIT

HORIZONTAL
SELECT LINES

VERTICAL SELECT LINES

Each core is threaded by three wires. The vertical and horizontal wires hold the cores at a 45-degree angle to the grid. A third wire is strung along the diagonals in a long wriggly loop. The core is addressed by sending current through one vertical and one horizontal wire. A magnetic change takes place only in the core located at the intersection of the two wires. If only one wire going through a core receives current, the core is unaffected, so the other cores remain unchanged by the address currents. The change at the intersection is then picked up by the sensing wire which can tell whether the core had been magnetized one way (a 1) or the other (a 0). Only one core in the array can be addressed at one time, so a second array would be devoted to the second bit, and so on. Eight such arrays of cores would give us the eight bits we need for our byte, and eight arrays of 64 columns by 64 rows would store 4,096 bytes.

When in operation the core control circuit first receives an address that determines which vertical and which horizontal wire locates the desired core. Read currents are sent through the selected wires, and the sensing wire then sends back the message as to whether the core held a 1 or a 0.

Jargon note: 4,096 bytes are called a 4K memory, meaning four thousand (approximately) bytes of storage. The convention of ignoring those extra few bytes is continued throughout.

1K = 1,024 bytes
2K = 2,048 bytes
4K = 4,096 bytes
8K = 8,192 bytes
16K = 16,384 bytes
32K = 32,768 bytes
64K = 65,536 bytes

Core memory has several interesting advantages. It offers fairly high-speed access to all its address locations. It is a permanent memory; it will not disappear when the power is turned off because the cores remain magnetized. But stringing together thousands of the little doughnuts and then soldering wires to connectors at the edges is a painstaking job that offers little opportunity for automation. So core was expensive, though not excessively so, when compared to the other costs of computer components of the same period.

You will not see many core memories around these days except in surplus stores, but many old-line computer people still refer to all electronic memory as core.

RANDOM-ACCESS MEMORY

When computer people talk about random-access memory, they generally mean an electronic memory in which the bits are stored in transistors on a Large-Scale Integrated Circuit (LSIC). Single chips are now marketed which can store as many as 16,384 bits. That is 2,048 bytes or 2K on one chip. As with core memory, the transistors are arranged in an array of columns and rows, and a specific bit is located by the intersection of a chosen column with a chosen row.

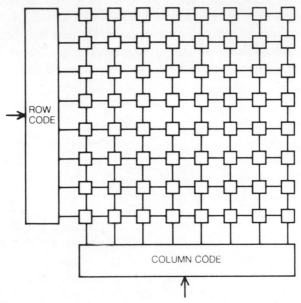

Remember that for the address we need a binary number large enough to provide a unique pattern for all the memory locations. An eight-bit byte will give us only 256 memory locations. Two bytes will identify 65,536 memory locations. We could theoretically have 32 2K chips in our random-access memory and still be able to handle all addresses with just the two bytes. However, housekeeping chores, such as telling the memory whether it is to read or write, will reduce the amount of memory that can be located with a two-byte address to half or less.

An 8K memory, which includes four chips and associated control circuitry, costs about $250 at retail. Most small computers have 2 to 4K of random-access memory. It is expected that 8K chips or larger ones, on 32K or even 64K boards, will be retailing for about $100 in the next ten years.

It will be helpful to see how the memory cell in the array actually stores the bit, and to do this we have to understand something about the operation of an electronic component called a capacitor. You have probably heard the old cliché about like things repelling and unlike things attracting each other. I am not sure whether this is true of people, but it is certainly true of magnetism and electric charges. It is this effect that appears in a capacitor which consists of two parallel planes of metal separated by an insulating layer of some kind—sometimes simply air, more often waxed paper or the plastic of an integrated circuit.

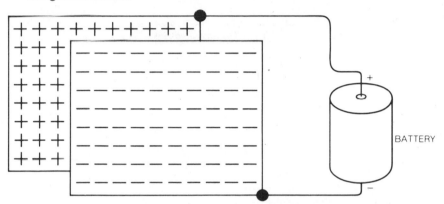

BATTERY

If you attach the terminals of a battery to the two plates, the plate connected to the positive terminal will collect a positive charge and the one to the other a negative charge. The two plates attract each other's charge to their near surfaces. Then if you disconnect the battery wires, the charges are trapped on the plates and will remain there more or less indefinitely, depending on the insulating ability of the material between them. If there is air between the two plates and you move them closer and closer together, at some point the charge becomes strong enough to jump the gap, and a spark will fly between the plates, allowing the charges to flow freely. This happens to people in cold weather and heated homes—the superdry air is a good insulator and makes it possible to accumulate a charge on your body when you rub your feet against a wool rug. Then when you touch an electric switch outlet or another person, sparks will fly as the charges equalize.

The capacitor therefore has the ability to store an electric charge for a time. One form of random-access memory uses, as its memory storage cell, a tiny capacitor built into the surface of a chip whose charge is controlled by a transistor.

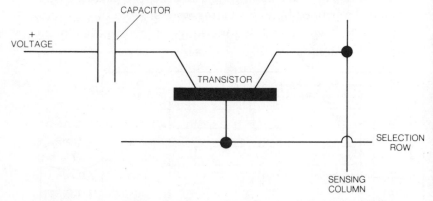

Here is one cell in the array of an electronic memory. When the row wire receives a positive voltage the transistor conducts, and the charge stored in the capacitor is connected to the column wire. If this column wire has been selected as the address to be read, the charge is transmitted out as a data bit. If there is no charge on the capacitor, the same connection takes place, but the column line receives no charge and reads the cell as a 0 bit.

We have to add several circuits to this simple array. The insulating ability of the capacitor is not perfect and the charge will leak away, so to keep the capacitor charged it is continually recharged by a "refresh" circuit which checks all the capacitors in turn and boosts the charge to the proper level at frequent intervals. "Frequent" turns out to be about 500 times every second—though this is only once every 8,000 clock cycles of the 4,000,000-cycle-per-second central processing unit.

Random-access memories can be made with two or three transistors in every cell. They obviously cost more, but they either take care of this refresh operation individually, or they are designed without capacitors so no refresh is needed at all. These are called "static" memories to distinguish them from the "dynamic" memories that do require refreshing. Static memories cost a little more than dynamic memories, require more power, and are more reliable, so at present they are preferred for small computers. Newer static memories are coming along which reduce power consumption almost to a negligible value. This is a very significant development as we will see in a minute.

A second important disadvantage of random-access memories is that they forget what had been stored there as soon as the power is turned off. Now it is true that there is no particular danger in leaving the computer turned on all the time. It normally draws less current than a color television set—but even that is a waste of energy, and most of us are rightfully uneasy about leaving an appliance on when there is no one around to attend it. In any case a temporary disruption of electric service would be sufficient to lose whatever had been stored, and if the information there is valuable, we cannot rely on house power lines. But if static memories will be available at reasonable cost, and their power consumption is reduced to the point where a standby set of rechargeable batteries can do the job, we can keep the static memory up and running 24 hours a day, even though the main power supply has been turned off. Rechargeable batteries can be built right into the memory board and draw their charging current from the power bus when the computer is on. When off, the battery would automatically take up the maintenance load and could presumably keep the memory intact for months and maybe years.

READ-ONLY MEMORIES

A random-access memory made with transistors can store a new bit or deliver one previously stored. However, many programs are used over and over again and will rarely if ever need to be changed. In that case we would use something called a read-only memory (jargon: ROM).

For a read-only memory we replace the capacitor in the one-transistor circuit with a soft-metal link which will melt away if a heavy current is sent through it. If the connection is direct to the plus voltage line, the cell stores a 1. If it is unconnected, the cell stores a 0.

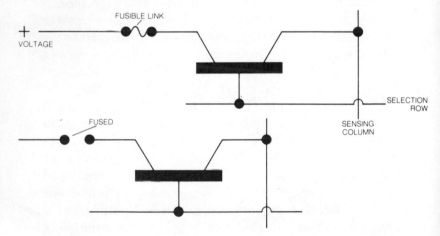

Fuses in home power circuits are made with such links that melt away when the current exceeds some safe value. In the read-only memory the chip is made with fusible links in every cell. When the desired program is decided on, a heavy flow of current is pushed through those cells in which the bit to be stored is a 0. The links melt away, leaving the desired memory in storage.

Once the link is gone the cell can never again store a 1, so new data cannot be written—hence the name read-only memory. The equipment to provide the fusing currents is specialized, and few computer owners are likely to have it. Instead, the manufacturer of the read-only memory either does the programming or else hires a company that specializes in providing programming before selling the equipment to users. A factory-programmed read-only memory is (in jargon) a PROM.

Note that read-only memories are permanent records which do not lose their data when power is disconnected. They offer high-speed random-access and so have important advantages. In many respects the read-only memory is like the prerecorded tape of a favorite piece of music. Whenever you want to play that music, you just slip the cassette into the recorder. Unfortunately programmable read-only memories are not in the same relative price class as tape cassettes, so unless it is a program you will be using very frequently, it is not economical to store data that way.

ERASABLE READ-ONLY MEMORY

Recognizing the limitations of the read-only memory, engineers came up with erasable programmable read-only memory (EPROM). This is something you might call a read-mostly memory. The assumption is that you will practically always be reading from this memory and will want to write or make a change at rare intervals. Here the integrated circuit has two gates for every transistor in the cells. The gates also act like two plates in a three-plate capacitor, the third being the silicon itself. One gate is permanently isolated from everything by a silicon dioxide shell which is almost a perfect insulator. Only a fairly high voltage on the control gate will force a small charge to leak through the silicon dioxide. The charge then remains on the floating gate for years. This charge permanently lifts the gate voltage, and the transistor remains conductive at all times. Obviously, if no charge is built up on the floating gate, the transistor remains off.

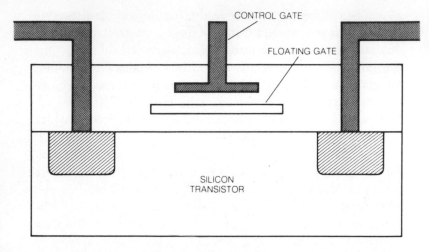

The interesting effect here is that the charge on the floating gate can be removed by exposing the chip to a strong ultraviolet light which temporarily makes the silicon dioxide conductive enough to allow the charge to leak away. The entire chip is discharged at the same time—selective exposure to the ultraviolet is a little tricky since the cells are tiny. The program is stored in the memory by selectively applying the desired charging voltages cell by cell.

In all of these erasable programmable read-only memories the problem is that programming is not done by the computer but by separate equipment. It is easy to spend $400 to $800 for a read-only memory and $1,000 or more for an erasable read-only memory.

SERIAL ACCESS

If you can do without strict random access to the data, you open a whole range of new possibilities. Some memory has to be at the speed of the central processing unit. It is useless to have a central processing unit that operates at 4 million cycles per second if the data on which it is to work can't be retrieved at comparable speeds. Random-access memories provide this speed, but if you can wait a few seconds the storage cost can be reduced dramatically. If you can wait a few minutes, the storage cost really gets down to manageable levels. For example, the numbers and characters that are output from the computer to appear on your display screen have to be held there for billions of cycles of clock time. A memory to hold those characters can be very slow in access time without causing any inconvenience to the user. In general, data that are to be read or otherwise used by humans can be put into a memory with far slower access times than those to be used by the central processing unit.

There are medium-speed memories under development that offer small size, low cost, and retrieval times of just a few clock cycles. Charge-coupled devices (CCD) and magnetic-bubble devices are in this class. The reason they take longer than random-access memories to deliver data is that they work with something very much like the delay line we saw in Chapter 1. An array of 64 by 64 storage cells is set up so that each column of 64 cells acts as a separate delay line. A bit is put in at the top of the column and moves down from cell to cell until it comes out the bottom. Each move takes one clock cycle, so the entire trip takes 64 cycles.

The only time the bit is available for reading or writing is after it leaves the bottom cell and before it is reinserted at the top. Special circuits take care of this and also keep tabs on which bit is number 1 in the 64, which is number 2, and so on, so that the correct memory location in the train will be read when asked for.

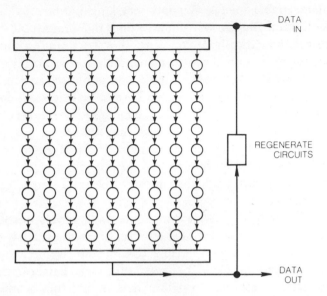

In spite of all the additional circuitry the serial memory offers a saving over the typical random-access memory which needs similar circuits in every cell rather than only one for every 64 cells.

The second type of serial memory is called a magnetic-bubble device. Here, microscopic domains within a thin film of magnetic material are controlled by magnetic fields above and across the film plane. If a domain is magnetized with its north pole pointed up, it can be considered a binary 1. If south is up, it is considered a 0. The domains are magnetized or reversed by wire loops near the surface of the film. Electromagnets alongside the film plane keep the train of magnetic bubbles circulating in a long narrow loop. At the top of the loop, when a magnetic domain passes a transfer site, it is read, written, or refreshed before being sent back down around the loop.

It takes about 16,000 clock cycles to access a bit in a bubble memory, but, again, this is only four-thousandths of a second. For the output purposes mentioned above it will work fine.

Another attractive feature of the magnetic bubbles is that, unlike the charge-coupled device, the memory doesn't fade when the power is turned off.

Computer people have a lot of hope for magnetic-bubble memories. While they do not compete in speed with the random-access memories, they may replace moving magnetic-surface memories which we will be talking about next.

MOVING MAGNETIC SURFACES

The best example of these is the familiar tape recorder—either cassette or reel-to-reel. Science fiction movies still show big tape drives to dramatize the operation of an otherwise unexciting electronic computer, though they are rarely used in modern computers.

All magnetic recording today uses as the recording material a thin film of ferrite powder. Ferrite is an oxide of iron which is easily magnetized, holds the magnetism indefinitely even when exposed to other weak magnetic fields, and can be used in layers less than a thousandth of an inch thick. It can be deposited on a variety of different base materials, and the bonding

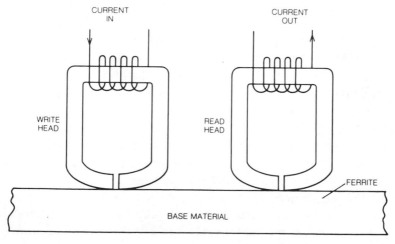

agent has fairly good wear resistance. Best of all, the materials and recording devices have been mass produced to the point where the cost is well below that of any other data storage medium.

A recording or playback head—and the same head can be used for both jobs—consists of an electromagnet with a gap that moves relative to the ferrite film. As current builds up in the coil of the magnet, the magnetic field strengthens across the gap and extends out through the ferrite film immediately adjacent to the gap. The gap may be only a thousandth of an inch wide, so the zone of magnetized film will be very narrow. When the current in the electromagnetic coil is reversed, the magnetic field across the gap collapses, creating a reverse magnetism in the film.

When a previously magnetized film is passed under the gap the moving magnetic field creates currents in the coil that are proportional to the strength and direction of the field. The currents can be amplified and detected, making it possible to read what was written on the film earlier.

It is important to realize that the magnetic film creates a current in the coil only when the field is changing—either growing larger or collapsing. This is why only alternating current can be used for magnetic recorders. Voice and music sound waves are also an alternating phenomenon. The sound waves strike a microphone which changes them into alternating currents which, when suitably shaped and strengthened by amplifiers in the recorder, are applied to the electromagnet coil.

Our binary digits are d.c. voltages for 1s and zero voltages for 0s, but it is not very difficult to add an electronic circuit between the computer and the recorder which changes a d.c. voltage to one frequency of a.c. current and a zero voltage to another frequency. Then one of two tones will always be recorded for the two binary states. Usually the frequencies are 2,400 cycles per second for the 1 and 1,200 cycles per second

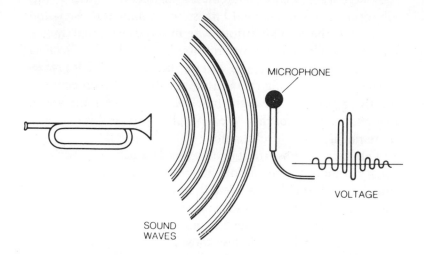

for the 0. This is called the Kansas City Standard to honor the conference which took place there at the time the standard was adopted.

Having dispensed with the first minor difficulty in adapting voice recording techniques for computer memories, we face a much more troublesome one common to all serial data recording. Our computer delivers its bytes in parallel—all eight bits of the byte come out on different bus wires. Magnetic recorders deliver and want their information in sequence, one bit after the other, or else they will need eight heads and eight tracks in the ferrite film. This means we need a circuit that accepts the eight bus lines, deciphers the coded bits, and then spits them out on one wire with the bits nicely lined up one after another. Also, some signal has to precede the eight bits announcing the start of a new byte and another signal at the end to announce the end of the byte. These are called start and stop bits. Sometimes other bits are included in the byte to make sure there is no slipup between the sender and the receiver.

A large-scale integrated circuit is available which will do this job nicely. It takes the eight bits, stores them in a register, and then sends them to an output wire in sequence, properly preceded and followed by start and stop bits and by the checking bit. It will also run in the reverse direction, receiving a sequence of bits, storing them in the register, and then connecting the register to the eight bus lines. We have some added cost and circuitry for this. We'll be talking about this circuit in more detail in the next chapter.

The last and most troublesome problem has to do with the serial nature of the recording. Suppose we have written a long program and stored it on a length of magnetic tape. The computer starts the program and comes to a place where it needs to jump to a new location for the next instruction. The tape recorder will need to run fast forward to that new location. Meanwhile the computer waits hundreds, perhaps millions of clock cycles. We are not just talking about a few seconds of waiting time. This could take minutes in a long program while the recorder jumps back and forth along a tape, exhausting the patience of the operator.

Disk recorders reduce this waiting time substantially, but the inherent serial nature of magnetic recording makes any of them a less than perfect mate for computers. The redeeming advantages of magnetic recording are first, economy—equipment cost of active storage can be less than $1 per thousand bytes. The comparable cost for random-access memory is $30 per thousand bytes. All memory costs are going to be 10% of these values ten years from now, but the relative costs are likely to stay the same. This means that by the mid-1980s you can expect to buy 64K of random-access memory for $100; a magnetic floppy disk drive might cost $100 to store 300K.

The second important advantage is that the amount of data that may be stored on magnetic materials is, for all practical purposes, infinite. All you have to do is remove one cassette or disk from the player/recorder and replace it with another. You can have shelves full of tapes or disks that will far exceed your needs. The storage is also relatively compact. An eight-inch disk, the size of a 45 rpm record, can hold 250,000 bytes which is the equivalent of a paperback novel.

While moving surface magnetic memory will never replace electronic memory, it has so many advantages that it makes sense to use it for those applications which don't need the speed and accessibility of random-access memory. What are these applications? Well, you could store a game you play infrequently, a Christmas card list of friends and relatives, an income tax computing system, or even your bank account records and read them into the electronic memory of the computer when the program is actually to be run. A very long program might be split in two with the first half read into random-access memory, run, and then the second half read in to replace the first and the program finished. The idea is to use random-access memory for actual operating time and the tape or disk for archival storage.

Jargon note: There are a couple of special words related to memories in peripheral devices like cassette recorders. These are "load" and "dump." Load is used when a program on disk or tape is run into the electronic memory of the computer. You don't just read the memory, you "load it in RAM." Dump is the reverse. You don't write your data into a cassette, you dump it. Loading and dumping are housekeeping file management while reading and writing are usually done while the program is running.

Loading time for a program will vary, depending on whether you are working from a tape cassette (say 15 minutes for a good sized program) or a disk (1 second for the same program). The difference is due to the density with which data are packed on disk or tape and the maximum speed at which the magnetic film is swept past the heads.

CASSETTE RECORDERS

Any good-quality cassette recorder may be used for computer memory, and for about $100 you can store data on ordinary blank cassettes. In addition to the recorder you will have to buy an electronic circuit which will convert computer bus signals to the two tone frequencies. Such a converter, called an "interface," costs less than $35; a recorder shouldn't cost more than $65 and ordinary blank cassettes run less than $5 each. Most small home computers on the market either include a separate cassette recorder as a necessary accessory, or provide it built right into the unit. These computers have 2 to 4K of random-access memory which wouldn't be enough storage to do all that is promised, so the tape recorder offers an inexpensive alternative. In addition, several computer manufacturers offer a selection of prerecorded programs on tapes. These include games, education, home management like pantry inventory or menu planning, and perhaps some financial-planning programs. We'll be talking more about these later. Right now we want to quickly review how the tape recorder works.

An audio cassette has a thin ferrite-coated tape which feeds through openings in the side of the cassette. The tape is contained on two spools—a supply reel and a take-up reel. The tape is $\frac{1}{8}$ inch wide and two tracks run along its length so that it may be played from one end to the other and then the cassette turned over and the second track played for the same length of time. Maximum recommended lengths of tape are 60 minutes per side. Though 90-minute and even 120-minute tape cassettes are available, they have a tendency to jam, and once jammed the cassette is effectively destroyed. Cassette recorders run at a standard $1\frac{7}{8}$ inches per second, and the maximum transfer rate is about 300 bits per second.

Special cassette recorders have also been designed and built for byte storage. These use larger cassettes that can run at 5 to 8 inches per second, and recordings are made with a higher

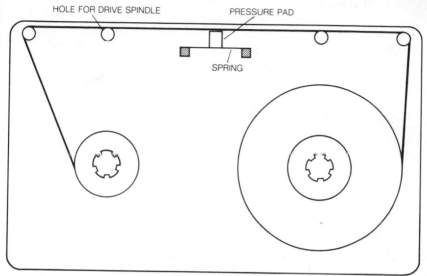

HOLE FOR DRIVE SPINDLE   PRESSURE PAD

SPRING

PLASTIC CASE

density of bits per inch on the ¼-inch-wide tape. Maximum transfer rate is 9,600 bits per second. These digital tape recorders also offer electronic control of record, play, fast forward, and fast rewind so that you don't have to do these functions by hand; they can be commanded by the program itself. Digital tape recorders cost about $200, and the electronic interface is about the same, so you are facing a $400 cost if you plan to buy one.

It is certain that for the next few years, at least, cassette recorders will provide the bulk of memory for personal computers. Their economy combined with their storage capacity more than compensates for their slow speed which, anyway, is not so troublesome in a home application.

FLOPPY DISKS

Certain kinds of data cannot work at this very slow access time but still do not need the electronic speed of random-access memory. The best example might be what is called information storage and retrieval. It is logical to put your entire address book on the computer because the central processing unit can easily cross-index each entry by last name, first name, address, friend through whom met, or any other convenient tag that would help you locate that particular address later. But it would be folly to put the entire list in electronic memory, and on a tape cassette it would take far too long to search from end to end.

Intermediate between the high speed of electronic storage and the slow speed of tape is a group of devices that might be called direct-access storage. The least costly of these is a floppy disk drive. Here the magnetic ferrite coating is on the surface of a flexible plastic disk about 8 inches in diameter and $\frac{1}{32}$ inch thick. The read and write head is held in contact with the surface of the disk which revolves rapidly under the head.

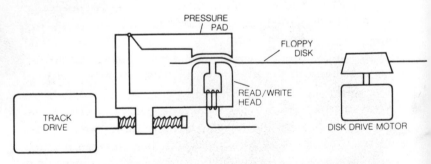

The disk is contained in a low-friction plastic jacket to protect the surface from dust and dirt—floppy disk drives are extremely sensitive to foreign particles sliding between the head and the disk surface. A radial slot in the jacket provides access to the surface for the head; a hole in the center allows the

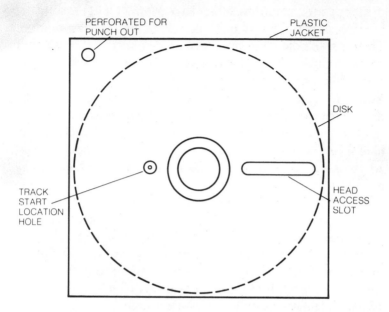

PERFORATED FOR PUNCH OUT

PLASTIC JACKET

DISK

HEAD ACCESS SLOT

TRACK START LOCATION HOLE

spindle to grip the disk, and one or more location holes in the disk signal the start of each circular track. The disk and jacket are inserted in a slot in the drive mechanism which then automatically grips the disk and spins it at 360 revolutions per minute.

The plastic jacket has a perforated circle in one corner that may be punched out by the user. A metal finger in the drive will extend through the hole, if it is knocked out, and throw a switch to keep the recorded data from being erased or recorded over. Recording is done in a series of concentric circles on the disk—not a spiral as in the high-fidelity record. Each full circle is one track of memory and there are 77 tracks on the 8-inch floppy disk. A smaller disk called a minifloppy or a diskette is $5\frac{1}{4}$ inches in diameter and can store less than half the amount of data of the full-size disk. Recently a two-sided drive has been introduced for the 8-inch disk with read/record heads on both sides, doubling the capacity of the disk and drive.

Floppy disk memories, either large or small, offer exactly the kind of storage that is most useful for personal computers. They can handle large masses of data at speeds that will not cause annoying delays in operation—about 250 bits per second. They are relatively impervious to user error or interference. No doubt prices, while relatively high now, will be reduced by mass production and innovative design.

Their high speed and storage capacity pretty much eliminate speed as an issue, but there are a couple of important disadvantages. First, the control circuitry is fairly elaborate. The head has to be moved over to the proper track. Once it is correctly positioned, the stream of data that comes out must be counted until the desired byte is reached. Elaborate address marks have to be placed in the data stream, and blank space must be provided to be sure that one batch of data doesn't overwrite another. Second, to position the head and hold the disk gets us back into mechanical drives which wear out and break down more quickly than all-electronic systems. Dust and dirt are a danger, and since there is rubbing action between the disk and the heads, eventually the heads will need replacement and the disk will become unusable.

Finally, cost is a factor right now. To incorporate a floppy disk drive in a personal computing system effectively doubles the price of the system. If you spent $600 for your computer, you can expect to spend another $600 to add the disk memory. If you spent $1,500, it is very easy to spend that much again for a good floppy disk drive.

PAPER TAPE

Paper tape is the tricycle of computer memories. Paper tape evolved naturally out of the IBM punched card used by early commercial computers to enter or deliver data. It is a long strip of thin paper, perhaps ¾ inch wide, and several hundred feet are spooled on a single reel. The tape has a center row of small holes down its length for a sprocket drive wheel. On either side of the center row of holes there is space for up to four holes on one side and three on the other representing the seven bits of a character. A hole in the tape signifies a 1 bit, and no hole signifies a 0 bit. Holes are punched into the tape by a pin that presses down through the paper and into a hole underneath. Holes are sensed by a row of flexible metal fingers that slide against the tape. If a hole is present, the finger makes contact with a metal pad on the other side, and the circuit is completed, signaling a 1.

Paper tapes have only economy to recommend them. They are messy—the punched-out paper circles inevitably escape the collecting box and spread through the room. They are slow, noisy, and, of course, permanent. Once the tape is recorded no change can be made though patches are sometimes used to correct mistakes. Also paper tape has a severely limited life since the paper wears and tears easily. For *very* temporary storage—if you don't mind the noise—you can consider paper tape, though for only a few dollars more tape recorders are far superior.

One new entry in the paper tape field uses an optical reader rather than mechanical fingers to sense when a hole is present. These are interesting devices for the personal computer because they are relatively inexpensive but function as fast as you can pull a strip of punched tape through the reader. Wear and tear on the tape is reduced, and the reading speed is dependent only on your arm length and coordination. Tape punching still remains the same slow, messy process.

5

INPUT AND OUTPUT

Computers work in a language and at a speed so foreign to humans that a large part of the cost of the hardware is in translators—devices that convert those quick-flying bits into alphabetical letters and numerals or the reverse. The devices that take our commands and data and make them computer-readable are called input devices. Those that take the computer results and make them people-readable, or use them to control other electrical equipment in our homes, are output devices. Computers thus can communicate not only with people but with electronic musical instruments, electric door openers, heating and air-conditioning systems, and practically anything else in the house that works on electricity.

INTERFACES

The computer does the translation with special circuits called "interfaces." The interface boards are plugged into a "motherboard" which has special 50-pin or 100-pin sockets wired together by the bus. Flat, flexible ribbons of conductors run from the interface boards to output connectors in the back panels of the main computer box (called the "mainframe") so that peripheral devices may be wired to their proper interface boards. These output connectors in the back panel are called "ports."

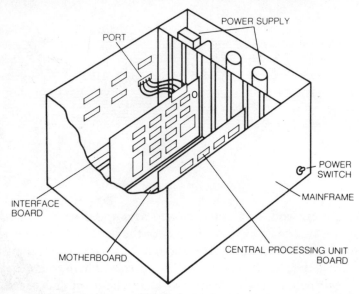

In the last chapter we talked about the problems of parallel computer output bytes needing to be turned into serial bits for magnetic recorders. The conversion circuit mentioned is on a chip called a Universal Asynchronous Receiver-Transmitter (jargon: the UART). UARTs are on most interface boards in the computer and in every input and output device as well. The UART is an integrated circuit which includes memory registers and logic circuits. The central processing unit delivers its byte on the data bus wires to the UART which stores the eight bits of each byte in a register, adds start and stop bits in front and behind as signals to the other devices it will be sending the bits to, adds a checking bit, and then puts the whole series as a train of pulses on the output wire. Actually it is a pair of wires, but one is the "ground" or "return," since all electric circuits must make a complete loop. The usual order of data transmission is start bit, data bits, checking bit (called a "parity" bit), and stop bit.

One of the problems the UART faces is that the computer is pumping data out at a speed no input or output device could possibly handle. The UART therefore has its own clock to time the flow of bits in the input or output devices in which it is installed. The UART in the interface board plugged in the mainframe will supply identically timed pulses. The standard UART clock circuit offers several different pulse speeds selected by switches on the UART board or on the front of the peripheral component in which it is installed.

The temporary registers associated with the UART are called buffers because they hold the bytes until the UART is ready to send them to an external device or to the central processing unit. In the usual mode the interface UART is first connected to a memory address by the central processing unit which then orders it to send the data found there to an output port. The UART takes the byte from memory and stores it in its register. It adds the necessary start and stop signals and then, one bit at a time according to the clock pulses, puts them on the output circuit. Data coming back to the computer are received in a similar buffer, and after the byte has been checked and the start and stop bits stripped off, the UART puts the entire byte on the data bus for computer processing.

The range of speeds can vary dramatically from component to component. A television tube display can handle data at 19,200 bits per second (the jargon term for bits per second is "baud"). At this speed the whole screen will be filled in one second. Paper tape punches and some typewriters can handle only 110 bits per second.

TELETYPEWRITERS

The slowest speed at which the UARTs operate is 110 bits per second. At this low speed the byte is traditionally made up of 7 bits for the character (remember that gives us 128 unique patterns needed by the alphabet and other symbols), 1 start bit, 1 checking bit, and 2 stop bits for a total of 11 bits. At higher speeds the byte is only 10 bits long. At 110 bits per second and 11 bits per byte we are transmitting 10 characters per second, and if word length is an average of 5 characters plus a space, we are transmitting at an average of 100 words per minute. This is the typing speed of a very good typist. Bits, bytes, characters, and words—let's see how all these relate:

Bits per Second	Bits per Byte	Bytes or Characters per Second	Five-letter Words plus Space per Minute
110	11	10	100
150	10	15	150
300	10	30	300
600	10	60	600
1,200	10	120	1,200
2,400	10	240	2,400
4,800	10	480	4,800
9,600	10	960	9,600
19,200	10	1,920	19,200

The maximum speed of an electric typewriter is around 150 words per minute or 15 characters per second, which is 150 bits per second. At this and higher speeds only 10 bits are used for the characters—1 start, 7 data, 1 checking bit (called a "parity" bit), 1 stop bit. Most computer typewriters, called "printers" to differentiate them from typewriters, can handle 30 characters per second comfortably, and a lot of attention is being given to raise that speed. So the most popular speed of UART transmission is 300 bits per second for a "hard copy" (printed output).

Teletype machines were the first to print characters in response to electric signals coming from a distant source or to transmit them to a distant source. The standard abbreviation for the Teletype is TTY, and it continues to be used for all computer terminals, though modern units are much improved over the original TTYs. One curious thing is that while input/output devices like the Teletype also create their characters in the parallel format used by the computer, they then convert them to serial format with a UART in order to send them to the computer's UART. This sounds like make-work for the UART manufacturer. Why not use the computer output directly?

The reason also explains the term "asynchronous" in the name of the UART. The computer is operating at 4,000,000 cycles per second which means it can produce 1,000,000 characters per second because of the four-cycle operating system. Only electronic memories handle data at that speed. If the data coming from the computer were presented at an eight-wire output bus, the typewriter would have to grab it on the fly and store it somewhere until it could get around to using it—the tiny amount of time during which the voltages are present on the bus is far less than the time needed to actuate a mechanical printing mechanism. Since a buffer is necessary anyway, it is more economical to convert to serial data and use a two-conductor cable between the computer and the peripheral input or output device.

Like all keyboard-display devices the Teletype has two distinct components. The keyboard translates a keystroke into an electrical signal to be sent to the computer. The typing mechanism receives an electrical signal and chooses the proper type bar to strike the paper so as to leave a printed character. If the output of the keyboard is sent directly to the typing mechanism, the Teletype is no different from an ordinary typewriter. The output from the keyboard may also be sent to an external memory, to another Teletype, or to some other display device. Since there is a functional difference between keyboard and printer, there can also be a physical distance. Keyboard "pads" are sold separately with only enough circuitry to translate the keystroke into a serial byte at the selected bit speed.

Keyboards normally follow standard typewriter format for the placement of different alphabetical letters and numbers and for many of the usual typing symbols. Extra keys are required for certain functions peculiar to computers. For example, the carriage return of the ordinary typewriter always advances the paper to a new line. In the computer keyboard the two functions are separated so that a different key is provided for line feed. The computer keyboard also has a break or interrupt key to stop the computer program when it isn't working right. The ordinary typewriter keyboard has around 60 characters—half produced by striking the key directly, the other half by holding a shift key down while striking the key. The computer keyboard has a second "shift" key called a "control" key which is held down while striking one of the other keys. This produces a third character for that key. For example, a control/Z (hold control down and type capital Z)

will, in most computer systems, delete the line you have just typed. These control functions usually do not print anything on the typing mechanism. They do, however, send a command to the computer or other device.

The print mechanism on the Teletype is a type bar that strikes against an inked ribbon to leave the character printed on paper. On the old Teletype the number of characters was usually limited to 26 uppercase letters, 10 numerals, and 25 or 30 special characters like punctuation marks such as the hyphen, plus, asterisk, and so forth.

PRINTERS

The limited character set plus its noise and slow speed have almost eliminated the traditional Teletype as the preferred computer input and output device. An adaptation of the IBM Selectric typewriter is the next fastest device to work with computers. Transmitter circuitry is added to the keyboard, and receiver circuitry to the print mechanism. Instead of type bars the Selectric has a metal-coated plastic ball with the characters raised on its surface. The ball turns on two axes to bring the desired character in line with the paper, and the ball then swings forward against an inked or carbon-coated ribbon to leave the character on the paper. The ball is very noisy as it swings back and forth, and it takes a fairly hefty motor to drive it at the necessary speed.

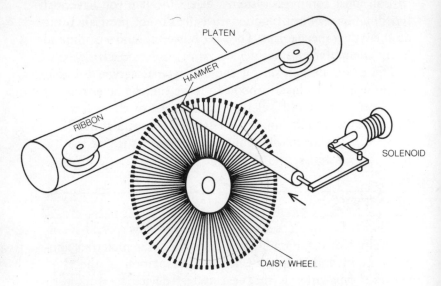

Other manufacturers have used different techniques to produce the desired print quality. In the Diablo printer the printing characters are at the ends of plastic fingers radiating like spokes or petals from a central hub. The "daisy wheel" sits just behind the inked ribbon, and an electromagnetic solenoid snaps forward like a tiny hammer to hit the end of the spoke against the ribbon and paper. Smaller masses are being moved, so the maximum speed of operation is about 60 characters per second, and the noise level is noticeably lower than that of the Selectric.

On both of these printers the paper wraps around a rubber-covered platen as on an ordinary typewriter. The "carriage" is the print mechanism—the ball in the Selectric or the daisy wheel in the Diablo—which moves along the paper, printing as it goes. The carriage snaps back to the start of the line after every carriage return. Carriage return (CR) or just RETURN is a very important command and the one you will be using most frequently as you program your computer. The computer doesn't normally receive your input until you have put enough information down to make it worthwhile. The amount is one line. You can type an 80-character line and hit the carriage return, and while your carriage is getting back to the left margin, the data will all have been sent to the computer which will be ready to respond.

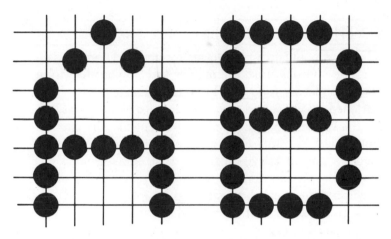

Unsatisfied with the inherent limitations of impact printers, designers have explored several other print mechanisms with varying success. Second in popularity is the thermal printer. This requires no mechanical motion in placing the character on the page and needs no ribbon. Instead, a coated paper is prepared so that when heated the white coating changes to black. The carriage aims a bundle of thin wires at the paper. In its simplest form the wires are in a rectangular pattern of 5 by 7 wires. A dot pattern is created on the paper when current flows between wire end and platen. By applying current to particular sets of wires, different alphabetical or numerical characters can be approximated on the paper. The more wires in the matrix, the better the appearance of the printed character. Thermal printers are very quiet since there is no impact and they can reach speeds of up to 120 characters per second.

Line printers are used when large amounts of data are being produced by the computer and must be printed at greater speeds. These have 132 or more individual print heads, and the entire line is printed at once. Sixty or more lines per minute are comfortably handled by line printers and the paper spews out of these machines like a waterfall.

CATHODE RAY TUBES

The most popular display device for personal computers is the cathode ray tube. Like the picture tube in your television set, the cathode ray tube (CRT) is an evacuated glass container flattened at its face and tapering back to a glass pipe at the rear. At the very end of the pipe is a filament like the ones in vacuum tubes, and this filament also heats a cathode (called an electron gun in television tubes) that emits a cloud of electrons. Moving electrons are what electric current is all about. Electric current can be controlled by magnetic fields so that the unfocused cloud of electrons that comes out of the cathode

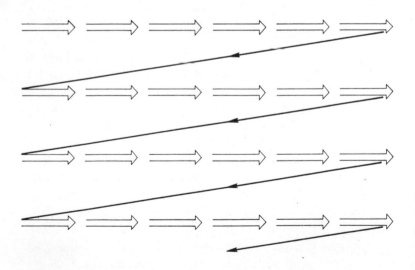

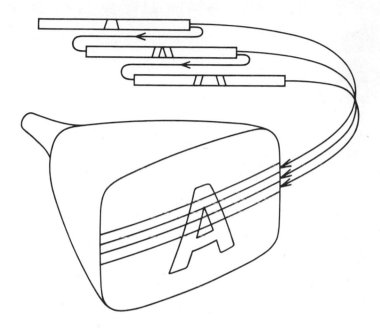

is shaped into a thin beam and aimed at the front face of the tube.

The inner surface of the face of the tube is coated with a phosphor which glows brightly when struck by the electrons and which fades slowly. The beam doesn't aim at one tiny spot in the center of the tube face; instead, the magnetic fields make it sweep a regular pattern across the face and repeat the exact same pattern 30 times every second.

To make a full frame the spot starts at the upper left corner and sweeps across the top to draw a thin line. It then snaps back to the left side at high speed and moves down just a fraction of an inch and sweeps across again. It snaps back again and again like a typewriter but with the lines only a few thousandths of an inch apart. When the bottom of the tube face is reached the beam snaps back to the starting point in the upper corner and repeats the pattern. The entire "scan" is completed in $\frac{1}{30}$ second—much too fast for the eye to see and thus giving the illusion of a constant picture.

Images are created on the screen by varying the intensity of the beam of electrons from zero to very strong, which produces a line with varying brightness on the screen. In effect we have sliced a picture horizontally into over 500 thin strips and then controlled the brightness at every point along each strip in order to build a picture on the cathode ray tube face. Each $\frac{1}{30}$ second a new still picture or "frame" is created on the screen. Each frame is slightly different from the previous one to create the illusion of motion as our eyes merge the sequence of pictures.

For computer output the cathode ray tube control circuitry is simpler than for television. We are not dealing with radio wave transmission, so we don't have to worry about coding our signals into the radio frequencies that will travel through the air. We have no shades of gray—either the character to be displayed is there with clear sharp lines or it is not there—so certain television controls like tuning are unnecessary. We do have a background intensity control which sets the overall screen brightness and a contrast control to set how bright the characters will appear against the background. You'll set these according to the light conditions in the room and your own eyes.

Operation is similar to that of a printer. The input stream of bits from the computer is received by a UART and stored in a memory buffer which holds the entire picture to be displayed on the screen. Each new character on the screen is added to the right of the previous character. When the line is filled, the electronic control calls for an automatic carriage return and line feed so that the next character is placed one line down and at the left edge of the screen. The location of the next character to be printed is indicated by a "cursor," which is either a little rectangle of brightness or a short underline to show where the next character will be printed. Sometimes the cursor is made to blink to call attention to its location on the screen.

Each character-byte (in ASCII code) is received by the cathode ray tube circuitry and interpreted as the particular character shape which is to appear on the screen. Capital letters, lowercase letters, numerals, symbols—whatever the manufacturer of the display has seen fit to include in his circuitry—will be written. The nonprinting characters such as interrupts or other control signals do not appear. Line delete signals will cause the entire line to suddenly disappear from the tube face.

When first turned on or when deliberately cleared, the display memory and the screen are empty. The first character received will be placed at the bottom left corner of the screen, and each new character will be added one space to the right of the previous character until the line is filled. At this point, or when the carriage return and line feed are received, the entire row of characters moves up one line on the screen, and the next character is added at the bottom left corner. It appears like a piece of paper in a typewriter in which the previously typed line moves up at each carriage return, and the new line always appears at the bottom of the screen.

The smallest character that can be clearly created for a cathode ray tube is such that only 80 characters on a line and a maximum of 24 lines can be displayed on the usual television picture tube. Each character is built out of the same 5 by 7 dot matrix we saw on the thermal printer.

When you have filled the screen and a new line of characters is added, the entire display moves up one line and the top line disappears. Some display circuits have memories that are larger than the 80 by 24 characters and you can "scroll" or roll the lines back as if rolling the paper back in the typewriter. Then some lines will fall off the bottom of the screen, but they are brought back by reversing the scroll.

This illustrates the two major disadvantages of the cathode ray tube display. You have no permanent copy of what has been displayed, and there is a limit on how much you can see at any one time. On the other hand the cathode ray tube is very fast—at 19,200 bits per second an entire screen of 80 by 24 characters can be written in one second—and totally silent.

There are three ways you can get a cathode ray tube display for your computer. First, it may be built specifically for that purpose, either separately or directly in the computer cabinet and with or without a keyboard pad. The built-in cathode ray tube, or the cathode ray tube used solely as a computer display though separately housed, provides the maximum number of characters that may be put on the screen.

The second way is to use a purchased television monitor. The monitor is like a standard television set except that it is intended for closed circuit applications. Monitors use what are called video signals. This is a picture in electronic form but without the radio frequency carrier that is required to transmit the message through space without wires.

To use a television monitor your computer must have interface circuitry that will produce a video signal. It creates a

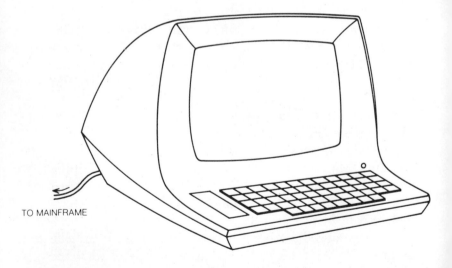

TO MAINFRAME

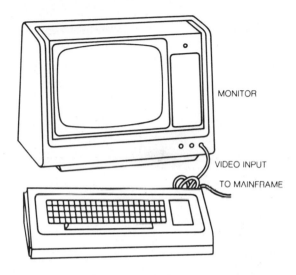

MONITOR

VIDEO INPUT

TO MAINFRAME

whole screen full of alphabetical and numerical characters and holds it in memory. It will have to refresh the monitor screen 30 times a second and, of course, add the new characters as received from the computer in their proper place. The monitor gives a reasonably good image—usually a maximum of 24 lines and 64 characters per line.

The last and least satisfactory method, although the most likely for consumer use, is to take the video signal from the computer circuitry and then add a radio frequency that will then permit it to be connected to the antenna terminals of an ordinary television set. Many of these "modulator" circuits do not have Federal Communications Commission approval because they may generate interference on neighboring television sets even though connected only to yours. In addition, the normal black and white television set (a color set is even worse) hasn't been designed to reproduce the tiny lines of small alphabetical characters, so the images are blurred and often vibrate and shimmer as other signals interfere.

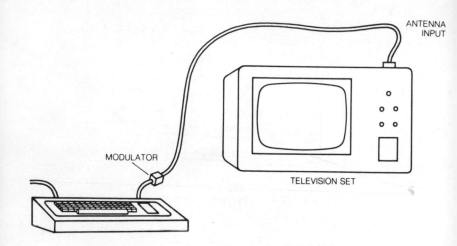

ANTENNA
INPUT

MODULATOR

TELEVISION SET

Some electronic hobbyists have modified an ordinary television set to function as a monitor, but this is a job for an expert. Be warned: attempting such a modification may endanger not only your computer but your life.

MEMORIES

We have written at length about magnetic tape, floppy disk, and other memory peripherals for the computer. These also act as input and output devices needing parallel-to-serial conversion but, in most other respects, are no different to the computer than the cathode ray tube display or the keyboard. The interface for a floppy disk memory will include the circuitry necessary to create the commands for finding a particular place on the disk, identifying it, writing or reading, and, of course, timing the bits so that they are sent or received at the expected speed. An interface for a cassette recorder will be simpler because the operator has to take over many of the chores of setting fast forward, reverse, record, or play modes of operation.

Some personal computers have a cassette tape recorder built

into the same mainframe housing as the other computer components. This eliminates the external cable connectors, but the same record, play, fast forward, and rewind buttons are controlled by the operator.

MODEMS

A self-contained stand-alone computer, which has all components built into one enclosure, communicates with its own terminal through very short cables. The coding of the signals is simple because computer, display, and keyboard were designed to work together. When computer and terminal are more distant, the signals will be sent through telephone wires, if direct cable connection is impossible or impractical. Then the signals have to be modified to suit the telephone system. The modifier is called a "modem" for modulator-demodulator, which means a circuit that takes the high and low d.c. voltages coming in a stream from the computer and transforms ("modulates") them into audible tones.

We saw that the magnetic tape cassette received a stream of bytes, each suitably sandwiched between start and stop bits, which the receiving circuit in the cassette recorder changed into two tone frequencies for recording on tape. Those same tones could as easily be sounded into a telephone receiver and sent through telephone wires to distant computers or from your computer to a distant display. For operating at a distance the printer or cathode ray tube display is combined with a keyboard to make what is called a "terminal," because it acts as the end of a communication line to the computer.

The parallel bytes coming from the central processing unit are made serial in the UART and then squirted out through a serial port which is now connected to the modem. Here a circuit changes the d.c. voltages into two a.c. frequencies which drive a little speaker built into the top of the modem. You can hear them as a series of high-pitched beeps that go through the telephone lines to the receiving telephone which sounds them at its speaker. A receiving modem has a microphone near this speaker to pick up the tones, change them into d.c. voltages, and send them to the display or computer attached to the modem there. Each modem has to be able to work both ways—receive sounds from the telephone handset and turn them into a series of d.c. voltages or take the d.c. voltages and turn them into audible tones that will be picked up at the telephone.

It sounds more complicated than it is. A modem is a small rectangular box with two rubber cups in its upper surface, which are sized and spaced to hold the telephone handset. You dial the number with which you will be communicating and then put the handset in the modem with the speaker end facing a microphone and the microphone end facing a speaker. When the modems are communicating, a pilot light goes on.

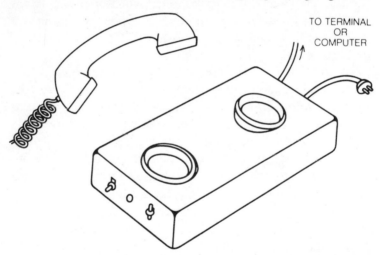

TO TERMINAL
OR
COMPUTER

The usual modem has only two switches, one to control the power that provides electricity for its circuits and one that selects "half" or "full duplex." Since separate circuits are needed for sending and receiving, it is possible to have a modem do both at the same time. This is called full duplex or, more simply, duplex operation. If only one circuit is to be used at a time the modem is set for half duplex, it will not receive while it is sending or send while it is receiving.

CONTROLLING AT A DISTANCE

In science fiction stories the computer opens doors, closes windows, starts dinner, serves it, cleans up afterward, and plays soft music to put you to sleep. All of these applications are possible, given an unlimited budget and a good bit of patience. Most such control functions simply require that a switch be opened or closed when some preset group of circumstances has been satisfied. For example, the electric coffeemaker only needs to have its power turned on at, say, seven in the morning. To control this the computer first needs a clock. We can provide a circuit for the motherboard which counts seconds, minutes, and hours, and when a certain time is reached, sends a signal to the central processing unit that a given set of commands is to be executed right now. The central processing unit interrupts whatever else it is doing and sends a control signal to the indicated output port that says, "Turn on."

Now we get to the problem. How does that message at the output port reach the coffeemaker? One way is to have every plug, every light switch, and every appliance in your house get its power from a monstrous switchboard at the computer. Each appliance would have its own port. When one of the output ports gets the turn-on or turn-off signal it actuates a relay that controls the current flow to the particular appliance or plug. It is possible that the house of the future will be built this way though it will take a lot of wire.

A second way to get individual appliance control is to put a receiver at the appliance and a transmitter at the computer port. Receiver and transmitter would then communicate by radio or through house wiring the way "wireless" intercoms now work.

A radio transmitter at the computer gets a turn-on signal from the central processing unit. It sends the order to the receiver just as your garage door opener sends a signal from the car; the receiver recognizes the signal, flips the switch, and the coffeemaker starts perking. Of course a different transmitting frequency is needed for each plug or appliance in the same way that a different frequency is needed for neighboring garage doors, or else, when the coffeepot is ordered to start perking, the roast might be popped into the oven or the front door answered. Transmitters and receivers of this kind are available. The transmitter plugs into the motherboard in exactly the same way all other interfaces do. It may need a special wire to connect to the house wiring, or a short antenna might poke up out of the mainframe. At the appliance end a little box is plugged into house wiring, and the appliance is plugged into the box. This is strictly an on-off control situation, and the computer will need a separate line of communication if it is to discover whether or not its orders were obeyed. The house of the future will undoubtedly incorporate devices of this kind.

DIGITAL TO ANALOG

For the situations where simple on or off control isn't enough, we have a new problem to deal with. We may want the volume control on our music system to be raised or lowered depending on the time of day and the kind of music. Or we may want lights to brighten as the sun slowly sets so as to maintain a constant light level indoors.

When we want proportional control rather than on or off we are back to the analog controls such as those we talked about in the introductory chapter. Here, voltage will take a value between two limits, and the intensity of the voltage will signify how loud we wanted the sound.

A digital byte from a computer is a series of 1s and 0s that symbolize a number, but it isn't a quantity. To translate the symbol into its intended quantity requires something called a digital-to-analog converter (DAC). This is a circuit which decodes a byte, determines the number it represents, and then sets up a voltage which is proportional to that number. The same device also has a reverse circuit which receives a voltage and produces a byte symbolizing the desired number.

One important difference between analog and digital signals is in the numbers of values between the two limits. An analog voltage can be anything from zero to, say, ten volts in infinitely small steps. That means it can take an infinite number of values between the two extremes. The digital signal is always limited by the number of bits used to symbolize the number. An eight-bit byte can take 256 values between the two extremes. Two eight-bit bytes can take 65,526 values. It may be that 256 values are more than enough to give the fineness of control needed, but if you wanted to shape a wave form for a musical tone in only 20 bytes, it is possible the distortion of the wave form would be audible. One cycle of an electrical wave might be cut up into steps like this:

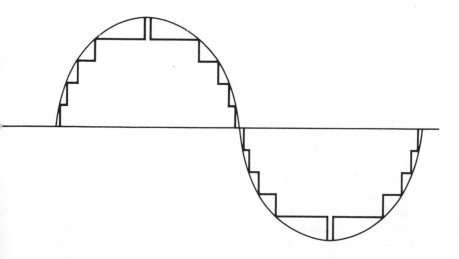

Digital-to-analog conversion circuits are available at economical prices. That isn't the problem, and it isn't that the computer can't do the job—present microcomputers can handle most of these tasks without the slightest strain. The problem is the translation of signals into control signals at the appliances. Our appliances are designed for human operation. There are knobs on your high-fidelity set, pushbutton switches on the blender, knobs on the oven, and knobs on the front door. Something has to replace the knob, something which can take an analog voltage and turn the knob shaft for us. Each appliance will need one or more such actuators and probably some sort of pickup—like a thermometer in the oven or a sensing device at the front door—to let the computer know that the desired oven temperature has been reached or that the front door is closed and securely locked.

That means our homes will have hundreds of little senders and receivers. I'd guess this is some years away, if only for economic reasons.

MUSIC AND VOICE

Even before there were computers, electronic circuits were being used to create and reproduce music. Mathematics and music have always had a strong affection for each other. While we think of music as an essentially emotional and evocative art form, it is made up of pitch (frequency), volume (amplitude), and time, all of which are completely definable in mathematical terms. Each note is played at an exact frequency, and the relationships of notes that create harmony are simple multiples of the frequencies. If you describe an amplitude and a frequency, you are defining a note. Even the different tonal qualities produced by the various instruments come about by the addition of "harmonics," which are simply higher multiples of the base frequency. Harmonics are what differentiate an oboe from a violin, for example, when both play the same note.

Music synthesizers have a keyboard like a piano, except that under every key is a simple switch like the contacts under the computer keyboard. Each such key is connected to a circuit that will produce a desired base frequency. Volume or intensity is controlled by a pedal. A series of knobs or slides permits you to add different amounts of the higher frequencies, the harmonics, to change the character of the sound but not its base note. You play the synthesizer by fingering the keys, and control the quality of the sound at the knobs to simulate real instruments. You can produce sounds never heard before because no real instrument exists that would put together the proportions of higher frequencies that you have dialed in.

A synthesizer is played in real time. That is, the sounds are made as you touch the keys. The synthesizer, therefore, requires that you know what sequence you want to hear and have some manual technique to play the notes in the desired order and at the desired speed.

Enter the computer. Now note selection, higher frequency additions, volume, and all the other variables can be preset. The programming time is separated from running or playing time. You can ask for a sequence of notes to be played at a speed faster than any human hands could possibly play them. You can make frequency jumps that go well beyond the limits of any given instrument. You can simulate the human voice and at pitches no human voice could ever produce. You can add more and more instruments to your orchestra without rehearsal or concern about how large the stage needs to be to include them all.

You are writing the music at your own pace, adding whatever complexity you want to the combination of notes, their timing, build-up, and fade-out patterns. Then, when you run the program, it "plays" the music through an audio amplifier and speaker after being processed by a digital-to-analog converter at the output because audio amplifiers are analog devices.

Music creation and performance by computers is a fascinating subject that involves considerable technical knowledge at this stage of its development. No completely satisfactory method has been developed to program the sounds—but that is only a matter of time. The fact that computers will free composers from the limitations of instruments and performers means we are going to hear very different music in the near future. A composer can write his music (program it), play, edit, modify it, add to it, play it again, and so on, knowing that each time he plays it the music will be exactly as he last programmed it. He is in total control of his medium. Not many art forms offer that much freedom.

THE TALKING MACHINE

Speech creation is similar to music in that it is also made up of frequency, intensity, and time. Speech recognition is another matter entirely. To identify speech sounds and translate them into printed English has proved to be too large a problem even for the largest computers, but we are getting close and the "voicewriter" should be in our homes within twenty years. When you think about the applications for a voicewriter—the machine that will recognize spoken words and use them to control a printer or other machine—you will see that it is the ultimate input device for our computer. It makes the keyboard obsolete. There is not a single function that the typewriter or computer keyboard performs that wouldn't be done better and easier with a voicewriter. In later chapters we'll see how it will be used with computers. Here, I just want to mention some of the internal problems voice recognition represents when used as an input.

Let's provide our computer with a microphone. Sounds picked up by the microphone are changed into voltages with frequency and amplitude, sent to an analog-to-digital converter, and then to the computer in a sequence of bytes that are unique for each phoneme (unique sound). Why can't the computer be taught—programmed—to recognize the unique pattern for each phoneme and simply display the equivalent symbol?

Well, since many phonemes are spelled differently, depending on the words in which they appear, how does it know where to put word spaces? How can it tell the difference between accents? We talk differently when tired and when excited. Will that confuse the patterns? Or are they unique enough to be recognizable no matter who speaks, in what accent, and how slurred?

Interface boards are available with microphones and speakers so that you can explore the limits of present technology yourself. The problem isn't in the hardware. We have the equipment to receive and record the sounds in all their infinite variety. The problem is in the software—the programming and the techniques for identifying what is unique about each sound. Human infants learn to do it in their first two or three years, but the capacity of the human mind is far beyond that of our computers. Does the human mind use a large part of its capacity to recognize speech, or has it just got a better pattern recognition technique than we have been able to dream up for the computer?

JOYSTICKS

Early aircraft were controlled by a "joystick"—a lever that stood up from the floor in front of the pilot. If he pushed the lever forward or back the aircraft would nose down or up. If he moved the lever from side to side the aircraft would bank right or left.

A joystick is a convenient controller for humans because it permits us to change two different variables at the same time and in one quick motion. Two separate knobs would offer the same function, but they do not suit humans as well as the joystick.

This then may be used as an input to the computer. Separate circuits for the two directions of control are built into the joystick and provide analog voltages that are converted to digital in the computer interface. Joysticks are the perfect input device for video games to move a "man" up and down or across the screen. They can simulate the controls of a spacecraft. They can simulate the aiming of a gun at a target on a screen or the speed and direction of a racecar as it follows a track.

Joystick controllers are available as little hand-held units with cable to the necessary interface circuit boards that plug into the mainframe. They are used exclusively for games right now.

6

PUTTING IT ALL
TOGETHER

A computer isn't a single machine any more than a high-fidelity set is a single machine. It is a collection of components chosen to accomplish one or more tasks or entertainments. The computer is probably the most versatile device since the invention of the book, but with at least two important differences: we can fill its "pages" with a variety of plots, plans, and ideas, and manufacturing techniques are still very much in the development stage. There is so much unexplored territory that manufacturers are going off in hundreds of different directions, each claiming to be the best, fastest, most reliable, and most economical of all. Whatever is true about what they say today is almost certain not to be true next week. With that as a warning, let's review the kinds of components that are available, which are essential, which are optional, and how they all work together.

THE MAINFRAME

This is an old computer word but it conveys the right meaning. The mainframe is a rectangular enclosure divided into two compartments. The smaller compartment houses the power supply. The larger contains the electronic circuit boards.

The back panel may have as many as ten plugs for connection to other components in the system. The front panel may have no switches at all, just a single power switch or a full set of toggle switches used for manual programming or checking.

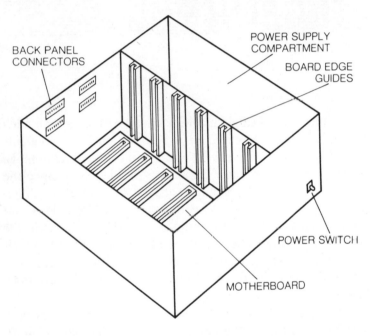

BACK PANEL
CONNECTORS

POWER SUPPLY
COMPARTMENT

BOARD EDGE
GUIDES

POWER SWITCH

MOTHERBOARD

■ *Power Supply:* This transforms the a.c. house current into the d.c. voltages needed by the other circuits in the system. Transformers, rectifiers, capacitors provide ripple-free direct current at 5, 12, or 18 volts. The power supply will have a

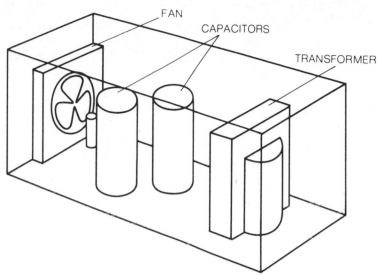

FAN

CAPACITORS

TRANSFORMER

built-in fuse so that if a short circuit develops in the system, minimum damage will be done. It will also usually have a cooling fan to remove the heat created by the fairly heavy currents in the power supply and to protect the other circuit components, since transistors and integrated circuits are easily damaged by excessive heat.

■ *Motherboard:* This is a printed circuit board in the base of the larger compartment in the mainframe. It holds and protects the 50 to 100 bus wires that will interconnect all functioning circuits in the computer. Ten to thirty edge connectors with up to 100 pins each are mounted on the surface of the board to take circuit boards.

The S-100 bus system, introduced in 1975 by Altair, has become something of a standard in the industry for the larger home computer. However, it is a standard being challenged by other manufacturers with smaller bus systems of different design. The 100-line bus offers all the connections one could need and more. Over a hundred accessory circuit boards are

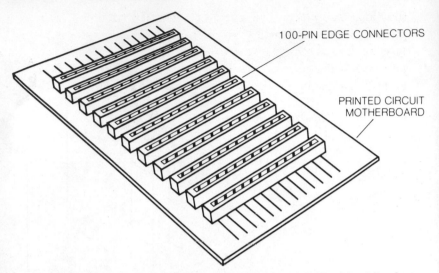

100-PIN EDGE CONNECTORS

PRINTED CIRCUIT
MOTHERBOARD

available from different manufacturers which will plug directly
into the edge connectors of the S-100 bus system, so this is still
the preferred design for the hobbyist.

Personal computer systems sold as assembled units do not
use the S-100 bus because it is larger, more costly, and more
versatile than needed by the average user. However, most personal computer manufacturers do offer extension adaptors that
will accept S-100 compatible boards, recognizing that most
users ultimately will want to expand their systems and that the
S-100 bus may be the easiest direction to take. Hobby computer manufacturers who do not adopt the S-100 bus are correct in their contention that it is not ideal, but the attempt to
force still other standards on the industry creates a problem for
the consumer.

The printed circuit boards which plug into the motherboard
are supported at the sides by plastic insulated guides for struc-
tural rigidity and to maintain the space between them for air
circulation and electrical isolation.

■ *Central Processing Unit:* An integrated circuit on a single
chip. Here, all the control, decision-making, and calculating

functions take place. The integrated circuit is mounted on a printed circuit board with the other integrated circuits necessary for housekeeping and connecting functions. The computer clock, for example, times all operations at 2 to 4 million cycles per second. The central processing unit board, like all

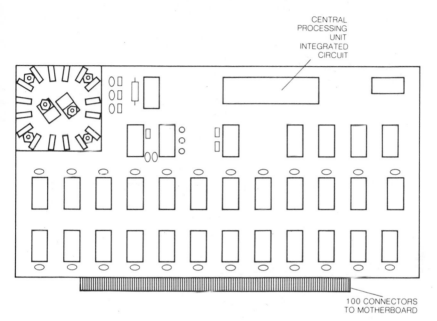

CENTRAL PROCESSING UNIT INTEGRATED CIRCUIT

100 CONNECTORS TO MOTHERBOARD

the others that will be plugged into the motherboard, is approximately 5 inches by 10 inches, with a row of contacts on either side of one long edge. These fit into the edge connector on the motherboard.

■ *Random-Access Memory:* Also called electronic memory because the data are stored on transistors or other electronic components. The random-access memory is on a printed circuit that plugs into the motherboard edge connectors. Memory is measured by the number of bytes that may be stored. Each byte is an eight-bit binary number, and random-access memory boards typically hold from 2K to 64K on a single board. Each

K is 1,024 bytes. Random-access memory holds instructions and data for the computer while it is actually running a program. The memory is lost when power is disconnected. It has the speed to keep up with the computer functions and may be expanded by the simple addition of more boards up to the physical capacity of the motherboard.

■ *Programmable and Erasable Read-Only Memory:* These are additional memories on boards that may be plugged into the motherboard. They contain fixed instructions or data sets that will be used often enough to justify the cost. Read-only memory will not be lost when the power is disconnected. However, data may not be written into the read-only memory by the computer while it is in operation, but must be physically programmed into the board by the manufacturer or with special equipment separate from the computer.

■ *Interfaces:* All peripheral (outside the mainframe) components operate at speeds or with codes different from those used within the mainframe. Interface boards make the necessary

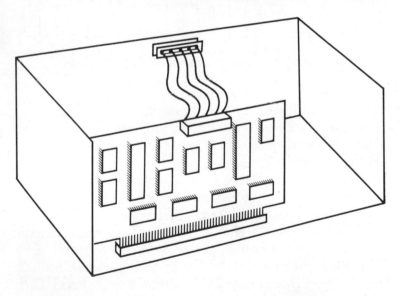

translation in both directions—going out to the peripheral device and coming back into the computer. These circuits are on boards that plug into the motherboard, but they also require additional connections to the back panel of the mainframe where the peripherals will be connected. Flat ribbon cables run from the tops of these boards to the back panel plugs.

KEYBOARD

This may be either an entirely separate component or combined with one of the display devices described below. At its most elemental it is a slim pad with a full set of typewriter keys plus additional control keys set in typewriter format on a top slanted surface. Contacts under the keys go to built-in circuitry, which translates each keystroke into its appropriate electrical code, and then sends the signals to the appropriate plug in the back panel of the mainframe.

This is the primary input to the computer. Commands, programs, and most other control signals originate here.

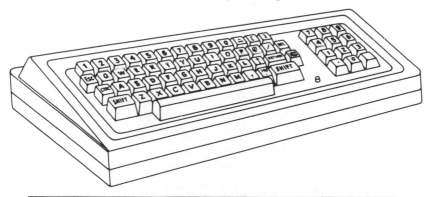

CATHODE RAY TUBE DISPLAY

A television picture tube used to display the alphabetical letters, numbers, and symbols that are typed on the keyboard or sent as output from the computer mainframe. The keyboard may be built into the same enclosure as the display, in which case the unit is called a terminal. Television monitors or standard television sets may be adapted to function as computer displays with or without separate keyboards.

TERMINAL

PRINTER

A typewriting device that receives signals from the keyboard or from the computer and prints characters on paper. The paper may be heat-sensitive for high-speed printing or standard for impact printing, depending on the specific machine being used. Printers operate at anywhere from 10 to 1,500 characters per second. Most personal computers do not have a printer because of the cost—a printer can easily double the total investment in a personal computer. However, many applications require this hard copy output, so there will be considerable pressure on manufacturers to design inexpensive high-speed printers for the consumer market.

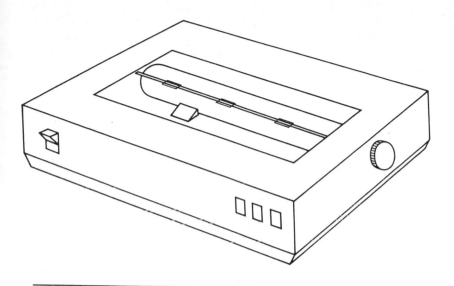

MAGNETIC TAPE MEMORY

An ordinary cassette tape recorder may be used for long-term memory. Signals generated by the computer and suitably modified in an interface can be recorded on cassette tapes for later playback. In this way programs may be retained for long periods of time without the expense of programming or purchasing read-only memory. Digital tape recorders are designed along

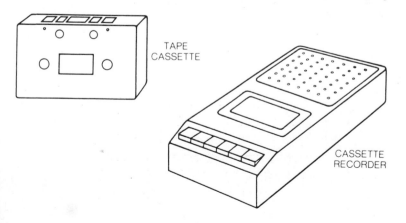

TAPE CASSETTE

CASSETTE RECORDER

the same principles as audio tape recorders but specifically for computer application. They will run at higher speed and may be commanded by signals from the computer to go into fast forward, rewind, play, or record modes. These functions must be manually controlled by the operator when using audio cassette recorders.

FLOPPY DISK MEMORY

In principle this is the same as the magnetic tape recorder. However, here the magnetic coating is on one or both faces of a flexible plastic disk the size of a 45 rpm record. A drive holds the disk and spins it at high speed. A read/record head is held against the disk and the data are recorded in concentric circles on one or both sides of the disk. Data transfer rates are slower than computer running speed, but programs can be stored here and loaded into the random-access memory for later processing. Each full-size disk holds 250,000 characters; the smaller minifloppy holds about 80,000 characters on a side. Cost is much higher than the cassette tape recorder but access speed is much faster.

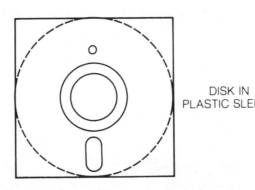

DISK IN
PLASTIC SLEEVE

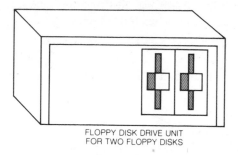

FLOPPY DISK DRIVE UNIT
FOR TWO FLOPPY DISKS

OTHER MEMORY DEVICES

Most low-cost personal computers include an audio cassette recorder for program storage. However, the cassette tape recorder with its limitations in speed and storage capacity may be only a temporary expedient in computer development. A drive for floppy disks will more than double the cost of the personal computer, so this remains a hobbyist's luxury. Punched paper tape is still in use and it is relatively inexpensive, but slow, and the tape wears and tears easily. Hard magnetic disks and drums work at very high speed and store very large amounts of data, but they are much too expensive to consider for private ownership.

New types of memory devices being developed include magnetic-bubble memories and charge-coupled devices. These would provide large amounts of memory at lower cost than other electronic memory and at somewhat slower speed, but will probably not replace magnetic memories for archival storage.

MODEMS

A modulator-demodulator (modem) converts computer output to an audible signal that can be picked up by an ordinary telephone receiver and transmitted anywhere within reach of a telephone. Terminals may, through this device, communicate with distant computers or other terminals.

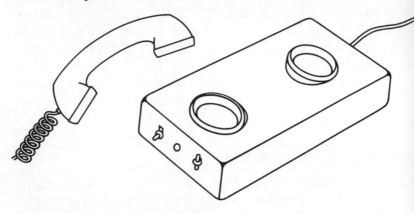

PERSONAL COMPUTERS

A term used to refer to a system that is within financial reach of a large market of consumers. It includes a mainframe with

central processing unit, power supply, minimal random-access memory, programmed random-access memory, keyboard, and cathode ray tube display. A cassette recorder is usually included with the necessary interface board plugged into the mainframe motherboard. Extra accessories offered by manufacturers include: additional random-access and programmed read-only memory; floppy disk drive; paper tape punch and reader; cassette programs for games, educational, and home economics applications.

PART 2

PROGRAMMING AND APPLICATIONS

7

COMMANDS TO YOUR COMPUTER

You have brought your computer home. It has a central processing unit, a random-access memory, a keyboard, and a cathode ray tube display. You want to play with it a bit before deciding what programmed memory you will need. You plug it in and turn the power switch on. What happens?

Let's trace the electric power into the machine. It flows into the input transformer to take the voltage down to the levels we will need for our electronic circuits; rectifiers then turn the voltage from a.c. to d.c. The proper d.c. voltages now appear on the bus to all the circuits. But the random-access memory is confused. There are small static charges remaining on some of the capacitors. In a truly random way some bit storage areas will take the value 1, some will take 0. The same is true for the registers in the central processing unit. Confusion everywhere—there is no consistent data in the memory; the program counter starts a long way from zero and counts meaninglessly. The clock starts ticking off its cycles, and stray codes find their way from the instruction registers to the central processing unit controller, which interprets them as best it can. Numbers appear and disappear on your screen in what is obvious nonsense. How do we get things started and under control?

You have to think of the computer as operating on two different levels. The first is what I call housekeeping functions—the orders that tell the computer what to do right now, in what they call "real time." That means things like, "Clear out all registers and memory and set everything to zero." Or, "Take this number and put it in register 1, now!" We will call these orders "commands."

The second level is the creation and storage of a set of instructions which will use the facilities of the computer at some later time to do a specific job. These orders are called "instructions" or "program statements" and the process of writing these statements is called programming. When the computer actually performs the previously programmed job it is called "running a program."

Though few books or instruction manuals about computers make this separation clear, I find it to be necessary information as I sit at the keyboard. We'll be talking about programming at length in the next chapter. Here, let's understand the commands—how to move the computer through its paces under direct control and in real time, people time, your time.

RESET

As we saw, when you push the power switch on you have no way of putting instructions into the machine, and it has no way of understanding the outside world. All it knows is what it finds in its instruction registers, and you can't get a string of instructions into the registers without help from the central processing unit which is receiving whatever random bits were in the circuits at start up. Do you see the trap? We have to build some self-control into the computer so that it is ready to go to work even before we turn the power on. Self-control is the critically important contribution made by programmed read-only memory. It is memory that is not lost when the power goes off, and which works at the speed and in the language of the central processing unit.

We have a RESET switch on the mainframe somewhere, which will clear out all the random bits that are in the circuits when the power is first turned on, and set all the random-access memory registers to zero. RESET is also the first command sent by the programmed read-only memory when power is turned on, and it is a signal you can use to stop a computer in mid-flight when it goes into a tailspin or gets trapped in an endless program loop and won't accept any other instructions. We'll see how that can happen later on and in the next chapter.

MONITOR

The minimum programmed memory you will need is called a monitor and, as the name implies, the monitor watches over the computer operations at all times and permits you to start, interrupt, stop, reset, and generally keep things in order. Right after you turn the power on, the monitor clears out registers, sets the program counter to zero, checks out any other programs also in programmed read-only memory, and turns to you for the first command. In most personal computers the monitor will let you know it is ready for commands by typing:

    READY

If your output unit is a cathode ray tube, a cursor will appear which tells you where the next letter will be typed on the screen. The cursor may be an underline, or a small rectangle of white against the black background; it may blink or remain steady. (If your output unit is a printing terminal you don't need a cursor because the position of the print head tells you where the next character will be typed.)

After the word READY has been typed on the screen, the cursor moves down one line and is at the left margin ready to fill a new line with your command. Depending on the particular TV monitor, you may also get a "prompt" character:

> >

or

> ?

This indicates that the computer has been cleared, the programming monitor, if any, is in control. Over to you, boss.

There are various ways commands are entered into the computer. Sometimes a single button carries all the information for a particular command. In that case the button will have the command or an obvious abbreviation printed on its surface. Sometimes you will have to type out the letters of the command entirely—usually not more than four characters in length. Sometimes the command is entered by pushing two buttons simultaneously. Most computers have one-button commands for CARRIAGE RETURN, DELETE, BACKSPACE, BREAK, or INTERRUPT. Some have a CLEAR command for wiping a screen blank. Some have a STOP button.

CARRIAGE RETURN

The first command you have to learn is the CARRIAGE RETURN, sometimes just called RETURN and, in the case of one personal computer, ENTER. You don't type this command in letters; it is a single key on the keyboard. Instruction books and other program listings will often print [CR] to indicate that the return button is to be pushed at that point in the program.

CARRIAGE RETURN is the command you will be using most frequently because it signals the end of any command you type. The computer will not start working on a command until you have signaled that you are finished by pressing CAR-

RIAGE RETURN. The first few times you sit at the keyboard you will probably type a command and then look at the screen for a minute or two, waiting while it just stares back at you. Then you will remember to hit RETURN and off the computer will go. Eventually it becomes so automatic you don't even realize you are hitting the key.

When you do type a command and hit RETURN, the command goes into random-access memory. As we know, this is temporary memory which will be lost when the power is shut off but, more than that, the command will also be forgotten by the computer as soon as you type another command (and hit RETURN). There are ways of preserving commands, of course, but that's really programming and we don't want to get into that right now. It is only important here to realize that the computer will not keep a record of the commands. It will accept your most recent command, act on it, and unless the results of the action have a lasting effect, such as putting a particular number in a particular place, there will be no trace of what it just did.

CORRECTING MISTAKES

The second most important commands are those that are concerned with correcting mistakes in typing. Suppose you want to change a letter or an entire line that was mistyped. You can't change it once you have hit RETURN, of course. By then the command has been entered and acted on by the computer. If it doesn't understand the command because you have made a typing mistake, you will get an "error message"—more about that in a minute—but if you catch a typing error before you hit RETURN, you will want to be able to change the character.

Different computers use different signals for deleting characters. Some have a key labeled DELETE or RUB. Some use a backward-pointing arrow or a key labeled BS (backspace). Some use "control characters," which are the signals sent to the computer by holding the control key down at the same time you type another character on the keyboard. Some control character signals are sent by keys of their own so that you don't need two fingers to send them. In this book I am going to show a control character with a C in brackets. For example, a control H will be written:

[C]H

Using this command will have the same effect as your BACK-SPACE key. The control command [C]M will cause a carriage return, but the return is also always on a key of its own because you use it so often. There are a number of other control signals that can be sent with the control button. The control characters don't usually print anything on your screen, but each does send a command to the computer which you may or may not see the effect of.

To delete one character you either press the DELETE key or the back-arrow key. What will usually happen is that the cursor will backspace and erase the one previous character typed. If you want to change two characters, you press the DELETE button twice.

Suppose you typed:

PAINT

and then as you looked up at the screen you realized you meant to type PRINT. Striking the delete key once produces:

PAIN

Striking it three more times leaves you with:

P

and you can go on by retyping the word correctly.

Some computer programs offer line changes as well as character deletes. If you have typed a long line and discover an error at the beginning of the line, or if you change your mind

entirely about the command you have just typed, it is convenient to be able to delete the entire line. Remember that if you
have hit RETURN it is too late—the command has been entered and recognized by the computer, and it has probably already been executed.

Small personal computers do not usually offer the line delete. It is a luxury you can do without. Larger computers which
you may be using on a time-sharing basis do offer it—usually
by means of a control [C]X. The action and response goes
something like this:

I AM TYPING THIS WITH A MISTE[C]X DELETE

What has happened is that when you saw your mistake you
typed the [C]X. The computer responded by immediately typing DELETE (sometimes a row of three Xs) and gave you a carriage return/line feed. The result is to put you exactly where
you were before you started the line.

THE PRINT COMMAND

Another important command is the PRINT command. The
computer will do practically nothing unless explicitly ordered
to, so if you want it to tell you the results of a calculation or the
status of its memories, you must specifically tell it to do so.
Suppose, for example, you want to know how much unused
random-access memory there is in your computer because you
are about to start a new project and want to be sure there is
enough room to accept it. You type:

PRINT MEM

or some similar command (depending on your computer), and
the computer will respond with something like:

3583

which means you have 3,583 bytes of random-access memory

unused at that moment. In theory, if you have a 4K random-access memory and none of it has been used for a program, you should get back:

4096

but some random-access memory is used for the monitor and other housekeeping programs, so you never have it all. The very exercise of being able to ask for a byte count means a monitor is being used, and that takes its share.

On some computers the PRINT command will also give you a direct read back of anything you write in. For example, type:

PRINT "HELLO"

and you will get back:

HELLO

Anything between the quotation marks will immediately be returned to you without the quotes.

One personal computer on the market has an internal clock which starts running whenever the power is turned on. When you type the command:

PRINT TIME

it prints:

001822

The first two digits are the hours, the second two the minutes, the last two the seconds. It is measuring elapsed time—starting at 000000 when the power switch is first turned on. This computer also permits you to set the time of day correctly at the start of a session, so when you ask for the time it will respond with a correct-at-that-moment time. You could write a small program to have the computer interrupt whatever you are doing and announce the time, though a separate alarm clock might be simpler. The trouble with the computer clock is that it will stop whenever you turn the power off, so the correct time has to be reset every time.

Most home computers will also work like a calculator after the print command. For example, you can type:

PRINT 263 − 124

and the answer will come right back:

139

The computer will handle all four arithmetical functions and powers and these can be put together into complex equations. There are rules about writing equations on the computer which are more logically discussed in the next chapter on programming; I'll remind you of this command then.

The PRINT command always requires additional information. It has to know what is to be printed. This additional piece of information is called an "argument" in a command or instruction, and in instruction manuals it is traditional to use sideways carats to indicate that an argument is to be inserted. For example, you can get the computer to work like a calculator with a PRINT <algebra expression> command. The bracketed <algebra expression> may be replaced with any mathematical relationship that makes sense. It may be

PRINT (36 + 93)/(8 − 5)

and the answer will be returned:

43

THE NEW COMMAND

To get started writing a program you must first wipe the random-access memory clean. You can do this by turning the computer off and then turning it on again so that the monitor program will reset (clear). You can push the RESET button yourself if there is one, but another way to get things cleared and ready is to type:

    NEW

which clears out the workspace (random-access memory) and makes the computer ready for a new job. If the computer requires you to name the new program before you get started, you type:

    NEW <program name>

The program name is any combination of numbers and letters up to a given limit. You might decide to put a one-armed bandit game on your computer. You would start off by typing:

    NEW BANDIT

Later, when you have stored this program on tape or disk, you can always call it back by its proper name. The NEW command is therefore an instruction to the computer to clear out the memory and get ready for a new program.

THE LIST COMMAND

All computer programs require that each instruction be numbered so that the computer will know in what order to execute it. These are called line numbers, and when you write your programs you will have to remember to include a line number at the beginning of every new statement. The line number indicates to the computer that it is receiving an instruction which is different from a direct command. A command is obeyed at once; a line-numbered instruction will simply be stored. Thus, if you type:

    PRINT "I AM WONDERFUL"

the computer will come back with:

    I AM WONDERFUL

If you type:

46 PRINT "I AM WONDERFUL"

the computer will store the line and wait for the next communication. Later on, when the computer is actually running that
program and it comes to line 46, it will print:

I AM WONDERFUL

at your terminal.

If you want to see all the instructions you have stored for a
particular program you type:

LIST

The computer will take all the line-numbered instructions, ar-
range them in ascending sequence no matter in what order you
have typed them, and print them out on your screen.

46   PRINT "I AM WONDERFUL"
52   PRINT "YOU ARE TOO."
98   END

The actual line numbers used are a matter of choice. You
don't have to start with number 1 and progress one number at
a time. As a matter of fact it is good programming practice to
start at some higher number—say 10 or 100—and go up in
tens—10, 20, 30, and so on. The computer doesn't care, and it
makes later corrections and additions much easier, if you have
lots of room between statement numbers.

Note that both the PRINT and LIST commands produce a
printout on your screen. PRINT gives you back the argument or
a specific reply if you have inserted an arithmetic function.
LIST gives you back all line-numbered instructions. In most
personal computers there are several variations of the LIST
command which permit you to print out a specific line or
group of lines rather than the entire program every time.

If you make a mistake while typing a line-numbered instruction, you can always delete characters until you remove the error and then retype to the end of the line. If you make a mistake or want to change a line-numbered instruction after you have hit RETURN, you do so simply by retyping the line number and the new instruction. Suppose you typed:

126 PRINT ''HO HO''

and then went on to other instructions. Later if you decide you want it spelled "ha ha" all you have to do is type:

126 PRINT ''HA HA''

and the old numbered instruction is replaced by the new one. If you want to eliminate the instruction entirely, just type:

126

When you hit the CARRIAGE RETURN the entire line will be wiped out.

THE RUN COMMAND

The RUN command orders the computer to actually perform the program as instructed. The three-instruction program listed above will produce the following printout if you now type:

RUN
I AM WONDERFUL
YOU ARE TOO.
READY

See the difference? When you enter LIST the computer simply repeats what had been stored. When you enter RUN it executes a programmed set of instructions. Given the RUN command, the computer looks for the lowest numbered instruction in its memory. If it finds nothing in lines 1 through 45 it simply goes on to the next. In line number 46 it finds the first PRINT command which it obeys. Then nothing until line number 52, where it finds the second PRINT command which it obeys. Then nothing until line number 95, which tells it the program has ended and it need not look for any other instructions. It has then finished its work and signals it is ready for more.

THE STOP AND CONT COMMANDS

Sometimes you will write a program with a logical error such as this one:

```
10 PRINT "HELP. I'M STUCK IN AN ENDLESS LOOP!"
20 GOTO 10
30 END
```

The poor computer never gets to line 30. The GOTO instruction (which we'll look at in more detail later) is really self-explanatory. It instructs the computer to jump backward to line 10, contrary to the usual procedure. In line 10 the PRINT command is found and obeyed, and the next step to line 20 throws us back around the loop again. When run, the result is:

```
HELP. I'M STUCK IN AN ENDLESS LOOP!
HELP. I'M STUCK IN AN ENDLESS LOOP!
HELP. I'M STUCK IN AN ENDLESS LOOP!
HELP. I'M STUCK IN AN ENDLESS LOOP!
```

and it will go on this way until you stop it. One way to stop it is to turn off the power, but then you lose the entire program as written. In this example it is no great loss, but in others, you may not be overjoyed to have a program wiped out.

The solution is provided by one of two buttons labeled BREAK, or INTERRUPT, and STOP, depending on the computer. BREAK or INTERRUPT will halt program execution and return the computer to the READY condition. This puts you back where you were just before you typed RUN. STOP usually halts the program in its tracks. You can then examine the printout, if any, up to that point and then type CONT for continue. For most personal computers CONT is the only command that may follow STOP. You can make no program changes or command changes when the STOP button is pushed because the computer is simply holding in the middle of the execution of a given program. The only other alternatives are to hit the RESET button or turn the power off.

So we have five more commands to remember: LIST prints out the written line-numbered program. RUN actually sets it in execution. BREAK or INTERRUPT halts a program while running. STOP puts a pause in the execution of the program which is ended when you type CONT.

STORING A PROGRAM ON TAPE

Now suppose you have written a program and want to run it for a friend who will be visiting you later in the evening. You can leave the computer running while you have dinner or read a book so that your stored instructions won't be lost. Or you can turn it off and write the line-numbered list of instructions on a piece of paper for typing in again later. Or you can put the instructions in a more permanent storage like magnetic tape using a cassette recorder.

Different computers have slightly different methods of readying the cassette recorder for the receipt of information, but the principles are the same. You need a clean, unrecorded cassette in the recorder. Previous recordings are automatically erased on recording new material, but unless the erase head is perfectly aligned with the record head, some small traces of the earlier signals may remain. Since it doesn't take much of a blip to ruin a program, all computer manufacturers recommend that tapes be erased with separate bulk erasers before recording a new program. You put the clean cassette into the recorder, close the cover, and make sure that the tape is at the beginning of the reel by rewinding to the end of the reel. Cassette tapes for music generally have a nonrecordable tape leader for a few inches at the beginning. Digital cassettes do not have this because they have to be able to record data from the very start of the tape.

You will want to set the tape counter at zero so that you will know where you are when the program has been completely recorded. Then a new program can be started higher on the counter without overwriting the first program.

You will have to attach connecting wires between the recorder and the computer—an output wire from the computer port to the recorder "microphone" input and a wire from the recorder "monitor" or "speaker" socket to the input port of the computer. Usually some connection also must be made to the control socket on the recorder that responds to the on-off switch on the recorder microphone. Then plug the recorder power line into house current and you are ready. You press "record" and "play" buttons at the same time. They stay down, but the reels won't turn until the microphone switch gets the "on" signal from the computer.

The computer is now in control but it doesn't know what you have been doing out there. It has a couple of new wires into its output ports, but it has not connected anything to those output ports yet. All it knows so far is that there is a set of line-numbered instructions in its random-access memory which constitute a program. Now, finally, you are ready to preserve the program. You type:

    SAVE

or

    CSAVE

or

    SAVE <name>

or

    CSAVE <name>

SAVE or CSAVE are the same commands for different computers. The addition of the "name" identifies the program so that later you will be able to find it among a whole series of programs on the one cassette.

When you hit the RETURN button, following one of these commands, the computer will start the tape recorder going and then feed the line-numbered instructions one by one to the output port going to the tape recorder. (On one computer an asterisk [*] will blink on and off while the material is being recorded to reassure you that something good is happening.) When the end of the program is reached, the computer stops the tape recorder and gives you a READY signal.

You now have the program stored in two places. One is on the tape cassette, the other is still in the computer random-access memory. Now you can turn the computer off and not worry about losing the program. Later, when you want to show your friend your new program, you will reverse the procedure. You turn the computer on and type:

NEW

to make sure any stray bits are cleared, even though the whole system should have been cleared by the monitor when first turned on. Put the cassette with the desired program into the tape recorder and fast wind to the starting number of that program. Then push the "play" button on the recorder (NOT the "record" button this time!) and type:

LOAD

or

CLOAD

or

LOAD <name>

or

CLOAD <name>

and the computer will start the tape recorder playing back. As it receives the signals the computer will transfer them to random-access memory so that again you have two copies of the program—one in random-access memory and one on the tape just played. When the end of the program is reached, the tape will stop, and the computer will give you a READY signal. If you want to execute the program now you type RUN.

There may be small differences in the sequence of operations depending on your computer. Sometimes there is a "prompt" command built into the computer program which tells you when to turn the recorder on. For example, you hook up the computer and cassette recorder and then type your LOAD command before pressing the "play" button. The computer will type out this message:

PRESS PLAY ON TAPE NUMBER 1

which you do, and the program goes into random-access memory.

ERROR MESSAGES

One lucky thing about computers is that if you make a mistake in a command, it is extremely unlikely that any damage can be done to the hardware. No sequence of commands, no matter how absurd, will hurt the machinery. But you can do a lot of damage to programs in storage—lose them, wipe out parts, put them out of order, put in instructions that you meant to put someplace else, or give instructions or commands that simply can't be executed. In that case one of several things may happen. For example, if you type:

PAINT "HELLO"

the computer won't know what you are talking about. It will say:

WHAT?

which tells you the command can't be executed. PAINT is not one of its recognized commands any more than RAN can be RUN, or LUST can be LIST.

You can also type LOAD and get a WHAT? The reason is that the numeral 0 is not the same character as the letter O to the computer. Your display screen will make that distinction by putting a slash through the number Ø and not through the letter. The typeset numeral 0 is usually a thinner oval than the capital O in most typefaces—but cathode ray tube screens don't have that subtle variation in type sizes so they use the slash.

There are many "error messages" built into monitor programs to let you know that you have typed a wrong command or improperly structured your command. The error messages are put in by the programmer who wrote the monitor program because he knows that typical errors will be made and that they should be distinguished from each other as much as possible. Sometimes the error will be obvious and you will correct it at once. Sometimes the error won't be so obvious. You will look closely at what you typed and see nothing wrong with it. Perhaps you accidentally typed a nonprinting character—like a control character. Perhaps the error is the result of a sequence of instructions that create an impossible situation. For example, you might divide by a variable X which looks perfectly correct to you, but earlier in the program X was set equal to zero. The computer can't divide by zero and it will tell you so.

Getting programs to run properly is called "debugging," and it is the most painful and challenging part of programming. The error message is only one indication of something wrong. Sometimes there are errors you will detect on your own. For example, the format of the printed output may be badly arranged and you will want to change it. Or the answers are obviously absurd by a factor of a thousand or more. The computer doesn't care if it makes no sense—only that it can follow its instructions to the letter.

THE PEEK AND POKE COMMANDS

If you do get into detailed programming, two additional commands will be useful and are supplied by most computer manufacturers. If you want to see what is in a particular memory location A in your computer, you type:

```
PEEK <A>
```

and the information will be displayed. If you want to change what is in location A, type:

```
POKE <A, B>
```

and you will put byte B in location A.

TEXT EDITORS

We now know that there are fairly simple commands to correct typing errors. These are called editing commands. But there are also text-editing programs available in read-only or taped memory which are much more elaborate.

Eventually almost everyone will want to use the computer as a text-handling machine. We don't really need a computer to solve mathematical equations very often—most of our mathematics is handled by others (our bank, the Internal Revenue Service, our employer)—but what we all do is write a letter to a relative now and then or invite a group of friends to a party or send Christmas cards to a long list of acquaintances. If your computer has a printer, you will soon be using it for these and many other text-handling chores. The very large computers used for text input by newspaper reporters have some nice features but none of the smaller computers do; this is a serious weakness.

What would a good text editing program be able to do? Well, you could examine large amounts of copy easily—perhaps by scrolling the screen up or down or flipping forward and backward through "pages," one screenful at a time. In a good editor you could single out a particular place on the screen directly, perhaps with a pointer of some kind, perhaps with a joystick control that swept the cursor around the screen quickly but with great accuracy. You could add text at that place, and the result would be to slither the rest of the text around in snake fashion down the page. You could add a single numbered line to a program. You could point to a character, word, sentence, paragraph, and delete it at the touch of a button. You could identify words, lines, or paragraphs and move them from place to place. You could search for a particular word or phrase, have the computer find it in the text, and display the page with the wanted word blinking or displayed in boldface type. You could scan the entire text at a controlled speed—fast enough to move it in a hurry, slow enough to give you the sense of where you are in the manuscript.

All of these are within the capability of a good text editor, but they are expensive in memory space and computer power. In the personal computer field the best text editor comes with the Commodore Pet which has cursor control that permits you to move the cursor left, right, up, or down one character or one line at a time. Once located where you want it, the cursor inserts new copy or deletes old copy as typed, and the computer closes up or expands the lines to accommodate the change. However, it takes time to get the cursor where you want it, and whole blocks of copy can't be moved or repeated in this system.

TO SUMMARIZE

It is convenient to have a separate list of the commands as a memory jogger when you know you need one but can't remember the precise form. Here is a reminder that may be useful:

POWER ON—a single switch which turns on all circuits, clears all registers, and readies the computer for input.

RESET—a separate switch on most computers serving the same clear and ready function.

READY—a "prompt" word telling you the computer is up and running and awaiting your commands.

> or ?—a prompt character saying computer has accepted last command and is ready for the next.

RETURN or CARRIAGE RETURN or ENTER—signals end of message to computer.

DELETE or back-arrow—deletes last character typed.

NEW—clears all random-access memory for a new program. Must be typed out in letters. Will not interrupt a running program as RESET, BREAK, or INTERRUPT will.

PRINT MEM or PRINT FRE—gives the number of unused bytes of random-access memory available for a new program.

PRINT "<>"—prints whatever was enclosed between quotes.

PRINT TIME—prints elapsed time from turn-on or from set time on some personal computers.

LIST—prints out all line-numbered instructions in sequence.

RUN—computer executes instructions in sequence.

BREAK or INTERRUPT—stops program being executed and returns to READY condition.

STOP—stops program being executed and holds it for inspection.

CONT—continues a program after a STOP command is used.

SAVE or CSAVE or SAVE "NO. 1"—records program on tape number one.

LOAD or CLOAD or LOAD "NO. 1"—plays taped program number one into random-access memory.

PEEK <A>—gives byte value in memory location A.

POKE <A, B>—places byte B in memory location A.

8

PROGRAMMING

In the early days of computers, programmers wrote long lists of machine language instructions. The programmer would have to know the hundred or so instructions recognized by the central processing unit and keep track of every memory register and its status as he moved bytes around and through the program. Some hobbyists still insist on doing their programs this way, and several computer manufacturers provide switches and input circuits that allow you to put in the instructions byte by byte.

Personal computers don't have input switches for the simple reason that programming in this way is a tedious and error-prone process, and there are easier and better ways to program. What we can do is to use the computer to write its own machine-language program from a set of instructions that are as close to the English language as possible. The instructions work like the commands we described in the last chapter—the computer receives one or more instructions and expands them into machine language. These instruction sets are called high-level languages and, like any language, each has its own vocabulary and syntax; that is, instruction words and rules by which the words are combined. The syntax includes punctuation as well as sentence structure. The only real problem is that while humans can understand a sentence with a grammatical error, the computer cannot. With some high-level languages, the computer will help you correct a mistake, but in others the computer will simply reject the mistaken instruction and give you no assistance in correcting or rewriting it.

BASIC

Just as every actor expects to direct his own Broadway play some day, so every programmer expects some day to write his own high-level language. Fortunately, there are only two or three languages we need to know about, and only one we have to learn. Anyone who has heard of IBM and computers has probably also heard the term "Fortran." The name is a short form for formula translator, and it is essentially a language intended for the handling of scientific formulas. The second language you should know about is APL (A Programming Language), a rather elegant language for mathematicians which requires many special symbols on the keyboard. The simplest and easiest language to use is called BASIC, because it has universal application for everything from mathematics to letter writing, and it is most like English in its instructions and syntax.

BASIC was written in the late sixties by John Kemeny and Thomas Kuntz at Dartmouth College, and is used by the students there in their course work. If logical processes have any appeal for you at all, learning BASIC will be a quick and thoroughly enjoyable experience. I will give you all the elements you need in this chapter, and while I cannot hope to make you into a proficient programmer that fast, you will at least begin to sense the power of computers in a way no other experience can duplicate.

High-level languages work in two possible ways. In the first you write your program in a high-level language line by line and then store it in random-access memory. You then run a special prewritten program called a "compiler" which uses your program as if it were data. The compiler takes the program instructions you have written and expands them into a machine-language set which is stored in random-access memory. The machine-language program can then be written into a magnetic memory device like a tape cassette, and your original high-level version can be cleared or erased. Now when you want to execute the program you call up the machine-language version and the RUN command. Note that two distinct computer runs are required, one to compile the machine-language version from the high-level language, the other to execute the program itself. This compiling method is efficient in terms of memory space and running speed and excellent for programs that will be run frequently as, say, a payroll every week or a mailing list for department store bills.

The second way a high-level language is used starts out the same. You write your program line by line-numbered line using the proper language and syntax. But now you can run it immediately. The computer examines each line, translates it into machine language, and executes the instructions at once. The computer then goes to the next line, translates, and executes. It then goes to the next line . . . and so on. This is called an "interpreter," and while less efficient in terms of memory required for the program and running speed, it provides the operator with the opportunity of watching or correcting a program line by line as it is being run.

In either case the program is written in a language that the machine cannot understand directly. A translation is made into machine language of either the whole program with a compiler or line by line with an interpreter. In BASIC we almost always work with an interpreter so that the program is run only once and stored in its original high-level form.

Several rules are common to all high-level languages. A program consists of a set of instructions or statements in line-numbered sequence. You may enter the instructions in any order you like, but each statement must begin with a line number. Statements will be stored in the computer in ascending order, and that is the sequence in which they will be executed. It is wise to think of the execution of a program as a plodding, step-by-step movement down the list of instructions. The computer knows nothing about later instructions while it is executing the current one, and it remembers very little about previous instructions.

Each line-numbered instruction is a statement. If you wish to change a statement, you may do so with the character- or line-delete methods we talked about in the last chapter. You may also change a statement by retyping the line number and a new statement. This erases forever the previous form of the statement and records and stores the new one. You may eliminate a statement entirely by typing the line number and pressing CARRIAGE RETURN.

Remember that whatever you wrote last into the computer is the only reality, and it is an extremely ephemeral reality—if you do not transfer the program to tape or other permanent memory before you flip the power switch off, you will have forever lost whatever was there. Even a temporary power failure can destroy hours of work, so be warned. Always save your programs if you wish to use them again and, perhaps, save part of a very long program if it has taken a lot of time to write and correct.

There are several "dialects" of BASIC currently available for home computers. The differences depend on the amount of memory available and to a lesser extent on the design of the computer circuitry. What we will be discussing here is common to all versions.

LINE NUMBERING AND END STATEMENTS

Some of the housekeeping commands we learned in the last chapter are also usable as BASIC statements. For example, the PRINT command is a vitally important programming statement, for without it we can never know what is happening inside the computer. Our first program:

```
10 PRINT "I AM WONDERFUL"
```

consists entirely of a PRINT statement. It is a little more professional if we add:

```
20 END
```

Most personal computers don't require the END statement in order to run properly, though larger computers normally do. However, it is a little more efficient use of computer time to include it. Without the END the computer keeps on stepping through (nonexistent) line numbers—and certainly into some other statements—until it reaches its capacity which, in the larger ones, is pretty big. In the small computer the END statement has an important protection function since you may also have other programs stored in random-access memory. Without the END statement the computer will run into the next program and execute whatever it finds.

If we wanted to be a little more elaborate, we could add to our first program:

```
10 PRINT "I AM WONDERFUL"
15 PRINT "YOU ARE TOO."
20 END
```

Now you see why we didn't number the statements 1 and 2. We could do it that way, but the computer doesn't care if you skip numbers and it is always better to have some unused line numbers between statements for later changes and additions. Experienced programmers generally start with line number 10 and proceed in increments of tens. Although line numbering is a bit of a nuisance, personal computers can take over only a limited part of that chore without giving up memory space, and memory is costly and more precious the further into programming you go. Larger versions of BASIC have line-numbering and -renumbering commands.

OK, let's run our program to see if it works:

```
RUN
I AM WONDERFUL
YOU ARE TOO.
READY
```

Neat? The first time you write a program and it runs correctly you will feel as if you invented the computer.

DOCUMENTATION WITH REMARK

It is almost always useful to be able to include notations and comments in your program that are not instructions to the computer but reminders to yourself or other programmers about precisely what you intended with each instruction. You will want these comments ignored by the computer when it actually runs the program. However, you would like to be able to examine them when you list the program and then study it to see how it works, why it doesn't work the way you expected, or how it may be changed to do something differently.

The REMARK instruction gives you this freedom. Simply add the instruction REMARK at the beginning of any statement:

```
5 REMARK THIS IS MY FIRST PROGRAM
```

Now when you list this program it goes:

```
5 REMARK THIS IS MY FIRST PROGRAM.
10 PRINT "I AM WONDERFUL"
```

```
15 PRINT "YOU ARE TOO."
20 END
```

and when you run it, it is unchanged.

Annotation of this kind within a program is called "documentation" by computer people, and they have a very high regard for programmers who include adequate documentation in their programs. Too often a beautiful and elegant program which you wrote in the past needs only a little change to make it even more wonderful. But when you try to change it you can't for the life of you figure out why you wrote a particular statement here, or what the effect of another statement is. It can take hours to re-create the logic which, with good documentation, would have taken minutes.

VARIABLES

Isn't it amazing that we have written so much about computer commands and programming in these last couple of chapters and so little about numbers or mathematics? Lest you think your computer can't do arithmetic, we'll see how that works. In the original Dartmouth version of BASIC you set up a calculation function with a LET statement. It goes something like this:

```
NEW
```

(NEW clears out the old program and starts us off fresh.)

```
10 LET A = 5 + 3
20 END
```

The computer will calculate the sum and assign the result to the variable A. Newer forms of BASIC will operate without the LET statement:

```
10 A = 5 + 3
```

There are a couple of things to note about the way the statement was typed. First, the computer ignores all spaces, so you can put the characters as close together or as far apart as you like. The advantage of space is to improve legibility. The disadvantage is that it takes memory space. You decide which is more important.

Second, the letter A is called a variable. It may be any letter from A to Z—so you have for small personal computers at most 26 variables to define. Larger hobby computers may add a single digit after the letter (such as A7) to give 260 more possible variables. The identified variable is unique in that the computer will assign a memory space to that variable and plug numbers or 0 into the space as the program progresses. If the value of the variable is changed in later equations, the old value will disappear and the new one will take its place. So while the addition looks the same as our old algebra, there is a difference. The variable A in this case has been assigned a value of $5 + 3 = 8$. It is not an equality in the same sense that we mean in algebra. For example, here is a perfectly legal statement:

    15 LET A = A + 1

which in algebra can never be true. The value of A after statement 10 was 8. The value of A after statement 15 is 9. The new A has been redefined in statement 15 as the old A plus 1, or 9. Most of the time this small difference in defining variables won't affect your programs, but there are dangers when you forget and use the same variable for two different purposes or when the same variable changes value depending on where it is in the program. There is also an interesting advantage to the way computers handle variables. A computer will let you use the same variable name two or more times in a program. If you reach a place where the old one can no longer be used, you can redefine it in anyway you like, and it will now serve a new function. It might be wise to put in a remark noting the change so that when you revisit the listed program later you will not be confused by the change.

Let's relist our first mathematical program because there are other things to be learned from it:

```
LIST
10 LET A = 5 + 3
15 LET A = A + 1
20 END
```

Let's try running it and see what happens:

```
RUN
READY
```

Nothing. Nothing happens. What went wrong? Didn't the computer follow instructions?

Yes, it did—to the letter. It didn't print an answer because we didn't ask it to. One additional statement is needed.

```
18 PRINT A
```

Now the RUN command produces:

```
RUN
9
READY
```

Note something a little different about this PRINT command. We asked for variable A without quotes. The computer correctly interpreted that to mean we wanted it to print the value of the variable, not its name. So there are two PRINT commands: one with, one without, quotes. The one with quotes gives us a literal reproduction of what is between the marks. The other gives us the value of the variable. Type:

```
10 PRINT I AM WONDERFUL
```

and you will get an error message after the run command. You won't get an error message until the program is run because all the computer does is store the statement in memory at this stage. Then when the program is run the computer will respond with something like:

ILLEGAL VARIABLE IN 10

However, the PRINT statement will accept a combination of variables and words if properly punctuated. Let's list our program and make a change in the PRINT statement:

```
LIST
10 LET A = 5 + 3
15 LET A = A + 1
18 PRINT "THE ANSWER IS";A
20 END
```

Now when we ask for a run:

```
RUN
THE ANSWER IS 9
```

Note that the PRINT statement here took what was in quotes and reproduced it, then inserted the value of A nicely spaced one place away from the "is." The semicolon tells the computer to put in the space. A comma would tell the computer to place the value of A starting 15, 30, 45, or 60, spaces from the left margin, whichever comes next. A period would produce an error message.

The need to use punctuation to help "format" the output (format means how the material is presented on the screen) is one of the annoying details in every programming language. We like our words spaced the way we would type or write them on a page. We like our tables with headings neatly centered over the columns, decimal points lined up above each other, and columns evenly spaced across the width of the page. Typists take a lot of time figuring these spacings and getting them just right. Nevertheless, it is a lot easier to do it than to explain to someone how it is to be done. In BASIC there are preset formats you can use with special punctuation—like the semicolon mentioned above. You can also specify your own format in detail, but it takes a lot of special instructions. I don't have the space to go into the subject here, but you will find it well worthwhile to learn the rules and conventions used by the version of BASIC on your computer and perhaps prepare a little table of definitions for yourself. It will save hours of frustrating debugging later on.

This also points up the need to be absolutely accurate when typing statements. It is easy to make errors in punctuation which produce disastrous mistakes that are very hard to find later.

ARITHMETIC

With two easily remembered exceptions, the mathematical operations are exactly the same as we had in high school:

+ means you add the two numbers
− means you subtract the second from the first
* is the symbol for multiplication (the × isn't available on keyboards)
/ is the symbol for division as in 3/4
^ is the symbol for raising to a power (4^2 is four squared or 16)
( ) are used to group operations which take precedence

The operations are performed in much the same way we do them longhand. Powers are figured first. Multiplication and division come next. Addition and subtraction are done last. The computer reads the equation from left to right and looks first for the innermost parentheses. It solves what is in the parentheses and then looks for the next pair until all parenthetical calculations are finished. Then powers are figured, then multiplication and division, then addition and subtraction. Here is an example:

    200 LET X = 5 * (3 + 4/2 − (1 − 6/2))/2 − 3 ^2

Note the multiplication sign (*) has to be placed before the parenthesis though it is "understood" in high school algebra. Otherwise the equation looks fairly standard. The computer goes from left to right and finds the innermost parentheses. Within the second parentheses it finds a division $(6/2 = 3)$ and a subtraction, so it does them and what remains is:

$$X = 5 * (3 + 4/2 - (-2))/2 - 3^2$$

In the outer set of parentheses there is another division, then the additions:

$$X = 5 * (7)/2 - 3^2$$

Now the power is done $(3^2 = 9)$ and then the multiplication and division is completed. In this case it doesn't matter whether $5 * 7 = 35$ and then $35/2 = 17.5$, or $7/2 = 3.5$ and $5 * 3.5 = 17.5$.

$$X = 17.5 - 9$$
$$X = 8.5$$

None of this is printed on your screen, of course. I just wanted to show the way the computations are made. Having finished its work, the computer assigns the value 8.5 to the variable X and goes on to the next program statement. It will hold this value until X is either redefined, or you ask for a PRINT including variable X in some way.

If you are using the computer like a calculator and write PRINT commands without line numbers, the computer will go through this same process and return the answer at once. It doesn't need a variable name and will have forgotten the answer as soon as it is printed on your screen. All the steps given above take perhaps a couple of hundred clock cycles, so the answer will appear almost as fast as the time it takes your cursor to get to the left margin.

BASIC can also handle six relationship operators:

= means equals
> means is greater than (X > Y means X is greater than Y)

< means is less than
<> means is not equal to
>= means equal to or greater than
<= means equal to or less than

These are very powerful decision-making operators when combined with the next statement we will be considering.

JUMPING STATEMENTS

Here is a short program which uses one of the relationship operators and a conditional jump:

```
10 LET A = 25
20 IF A < 18 THEN 50
30 PRINT "AL IS AN ADULT"
40 END
50 PRINT "AL IS A MINOR"
60 END
```

Line 20 says that if variable A has a value less than 18, the program should skip to line 50. If A is 18 or over, the IF-THEN statement would be passed over, and the program continues to line 30. The extra END statement in line 40 terminates the program there, otherwise both PRINT statements would be read and executed, giving us a nonsense response. The IF-THEN statement is a simple conditional which can use any of the six relationship operators listed above.

Another way of stopping the program after line 30 is:

```
40 GOTO 60
```

The GOTO statement is an unconditional jump. You have "branched" at the IF-THEN statement, depending on the value of A. At the end of each branch the program must be terminated, so we do that either by putting separate END statements or the unconditional jump to the END statement in line 60.

INPUT STATEMENTS

The program as written is really trivial because we start out by setting a value for the variable A as 25. Let's open up the possibility of A being many different values. Add one statement and modify one:

```
5 PRINT "HOW OLD IS AL"
10 INPUT A
20 IF A = 18 THEN 50
30 PRINT "AL IS AN ADULT"
40 GOTO 60
50 PRINT "AL IS A MINOR"
60 END
```

The new statement 5 is one of our standard PRINT ">" statements which will write out the question when we run the program. Statement 10, however, is very new. When the computer finds this instruction it goes to a fresh line (carriage return and line feed) and prints a question mark. It then waits for a response from the keyboard. When the operator responds by putting in a numerical answer, the computer assigns that number to variable A. The program operates like this:

```
RUN
HOW OLD IS AL
?_
```

And the computer now waits for you. If you type any number under 18 the computer will print:

```
AL IS A MINOR
READY
```

If you type 18 or any higher number (even 16,547!), the computer will print:

```
AL IS AN ADULT
READY
```

A slightly tighter way to program this combines lines 5 and 10:

```
10 INPUT "HOW OLD IS AL";A
```

Now when you run, the question mark is placed right after the text and the cursor waits on the same line for the response from the keyboard:

```
RUN
HOW OLD IS AL?_
```

REVIEW

It is time for a brief review of the statements we have learned.

Statements differ from commands in that they become part of a program and are not obeyed until the program is run. Statements must be line numbered, and the program will always put the lines in ascending order and print them out in that order when you command LIST.

PRINT "<>" returns the quoted material verbatim when the statement is reached in the program. PRINT X (or any other specified variable) returns the value of variable X. A variable may be any one of the 26 letters or a letter and a single numerical digit.

REMARK is a statement of information for the programmer and will be ignored by the computer as it steps through the program.

$+$, $-$, $*$, $/$, $\hat{}$, $=$, $>$, $<$, $<>$, $=>$, $=<$ are all mathematical and relationship operators. As with normal algebra, material between parentheses takes precedence. Powers are computed first, then multiplication and division, then addition and subtraction.

An IF-THEN statement is a conditional branch using one of the relationship operators. If the variable satisfies the relationship, the program jumps to the line following THEN; otherwise it steps on to the next line-numbered statement.

GOTO is an unconditional jump sending the program to the given line number. It usually appears at the end of a program branch.

INPUT X stops the program and waits for the operator to provide a value to be assigned to variable X.

INPUT "<>";X prints the bracketed material and then stops the program and waits for the value to be assigned to variable X.

LOOPS

The IF-THEN and the GOTO statements don't have to be simple branches which wind up at an END. They can also create loops within the program that really get the computer working for you. Here is an example of a simple, but dangerous, loop:

```
10 PRINT "OH, HOW I HATE THE RAIN."
20 GOTO 10
30 END
```

What do you suppose will happen when we run this program? You are right; it will keep printing the quoted line endlessly. This is one of those situations when the BREAK or INTERRUPT button is essential to stop the program. Now let's do the same thing with a little more control:

```
10 FOR A = 1 TO 10
20 PRINT "OH, HOW I HATE THE RAIN."
30 NEXT A
40 END
```

The FOR-NEXT pair of statements in lines 10 and 30 always signals the beginning and end of a controlled loop. Once it encounters the FOR statement in line 10 the computer sets up a new variable which you have defined. Variable A is a "counting" variable within the loop. The first value it takes is also given—in this case 1. The computer assigns the value 1 to variable A and moves on into the loop. It prints the quoted line and reaches the NEXT A statement which sends the program back to line 10. Variable A takes its next value, in this case 2, and the program goes on to line 20. It prints the quote for the second time and reaches line 30 which sends it back to 10 to take variable A up to value 3. And so on for the ten times. When A reaches value 10 the loop is traveled for the last time. The NEXT A statement is ignored and the program "exits" the loop and goes to line 40. The result is that the quoted statement has been printed ten times and that's all.

In this example the variable A was never itself used in the loop; it functioned as a counting variable and nothing else. There are loops when the value of the counting variable is also used within the loop, and there are times when the variable used to count with may have had some other function in the program and will continue to have a function later on. In that instance the steps counted in each loop don't necessarily have to be 1. You may write a slightly more elaborate statement:

```
10 FOR A = 2 TO 10 STEP 2
```

and now the PRINT command will be executed only five times as A takes the values 2, 4, 6, 8, and 10. Obviously any two limits and any steps can be specified. Even negative numbers may be stepped:

```
10 FOR A = −10 TO −50 STEP −5
```

will give you nine printed sentences as A takes the values −10, −15, −20, −25, −30, −35, −40, −45, −50. As this loop is being executed—at computer speeds—no output goes to the screen unless specifically ordered within the loop. Here is a nice example of how that may be done using our earlier program:

```
10 FOR A = 15 TO 20
20 IF A < 18 THEN 50
30 PRINT "WHEN AL IS";A;"HE IS AN ADULT"
```

```
40 GOTO 60
50 PRINT "WHEN AL IS";A;"HE IS A MINOR"
60 NEXT A
70 END
```

Now let's see what happens when we run this program:

```
RUN
WHEN AL IS 15 HE IS A MINOR
WHEN AL IS 16 HE IS A MINOR
WHEN AL IS 17 HE IS A MINOR
WHEN AL IS 18 HE IS AN ADULT
WHEN AL IS 19 HE IS AN ADULT
WHEN AL IS 20 HE IS AN ADULT
READY
```

Now we begin to see how to get the computer to do thousands of calculations over and over at breakneck speed. Suppose we want a table of sales taxes for every purchase price from $1 to $100. We create a simple loop that goes something like this:

```
10 PRINT "SALE", "TAX"
20 PRINT
30 FOR S = 1 TO 100 STEP .2
40 LET T = .05 * S
50 PRINT S,T
60 NEXT S
70 END
```

We are going up in $.20 increments here to show the tax in even penny steps (5% of $.20 is $.01). The commas in the PRINT statements are formatting signals. The first variable or quoted statement is printed flush at the left margin. After the comma the printing automatically tabs to the 15th space to the right of the left margin. Additional commas move the print head over to the 30th space. This makes tables easy to set up without having to do a lot of planning beforehand. The only other new statement that may look a little strange here is in line 20 where the PRINT statement has no argument at all. It produces a blank line in the output and improves the look of the table:

RUN

SALE	TAX
1	0.05
1.2	0.06
1.4	0.07
1.6	0.08
1.8	0.09
2.	0.1
2.2	0.11
2.4	0.12
2.6	0.13
2.8	0.14
3.	0.15
3.2	0.16
.	.
.	.
.	.

and so on.

Note that the computer automatically drops the trailing zeros ($3. not $3.0 or $3.00). In order to get two decimal places—whether or not they are zeros—you have to put in one of those special formatting statements, and for a dollar-and-cents table of this kind it probably should be included. Also the output has to go to a printer of some kind because if you output this to your cathode ray tube, it will very soon run off the top of the screen, and at the end you will be left with the last twenty or so items in the table. Once printed out you could post the table near a cash register. The program itself is so short and easily rewritten that you would have no reason to keep it indefinitely on tape.

Yes, there are lots of other ways to accomplish the job. Your computer could have its keyboard and screen at the cash register. When you ring up a sale you also use the direct PRINT and calculate mode:

PRINT .05 * <sale in dollars and cents>

or you would set up the program with an INPUT statement so that the computer asks for the value of the sale. Then it would calculate and print out the 5% tax. But the use of a computer to generate a look-up table is clearly the most efficient use of its time. If it must calculate a new sales tax figure every time a sale is made, you would be better off with a $10 calculator at the check-out register. I include the example because the idea that the computer would go ahead and figure the sales tax almost 500 times and then print eight single-spaced pages of table without a single typing error in four or five minutes (at the maximum print speed of 30 characters per second) brings home some of the wonders of the machine.

The speed and volume of the output presents its own problem of course. The listing is too long for a cathode ray tube screen, but you can build a pause into the program which will hold the images on the screen for a few seconds. It might be better if the page was written on the screen and then held until a continue signal of some kind is given by the operator (with an INPUT statement). You will find your own computer manual quite explicit about how to do these and other programming changes to make over-long copy readable.

ARRAYS AND MATRICES

We can't leave loops without pointing out that you can have a loop entirely enclosed within another loop. These are called nested loops, and they are useful for exploring a second dimension of some variable.

We have two new words to learn here. The first is "array," which is simply a list of numbers. The sales from $1 to $10 are such a list and can be called an array. Now suppose we wanted to produce a table which would take into account the possibility of an increase in the sales tax. We want a different array or list for each tax percentage level. $T(5)$ would be the tax at 5%, $T(6)$ would be the tax at 6%, and so on. The combination of different sales taxes at different sales produces a table of values that is called a "matrix."

Loops within loops define matrices. Here is an example:

```
 10  PRINT "SALE", "5% TAX", "6% TAX", "7% TAX"
 20  PRINT
 30    FOR S = 1 TO 10
 40    PRINT S,
 50      FOR P = 5 TO 8
 60      LET T(P) = S * P/100
 70      PRINT T(P),
 80      NEXT P
 90    NEXT S
100  END
```

Here there are two counting variables. One is sales, S, and the other is P nested within the S loop. The P is sales tax percentage and it takes only three values—5, 6, and 7. The inner loop calculates a different tax for each of the three values of sales tax percentage and stores them under the variable names $T(5)$, $T(6)$, and $T(7)$. Then before the next sales value is stepped the three tax values are printed on the same line as S but stepped over to the next column. Now we go up to the next sales dollar value and recalculate the taxes.

Here is how the table prints out:

SALE	5% TAX	6% TAX	7% TAX
1	0.05	0.06	0.07
2	0.1	0.12	0.14
3	0.15	0.18	0.21
4	0.2	0.24	0.28
5	0.25	0.3	0.35
6	0.3	0.36	0.42
7	0.35	0.42	0.49
8	0.4	0.48	0.56
9	0.45	0.54	0.63
10	0.5	0.6	0.7

There are several interesting things in this program. The inner loop takes each of the three values for each of the ten values of S. For easy reading the inner loop is indented a couple of spaces when you type the program. This is a good practice when you are typing your own programs because it makes the loops a lot easier to read at the cost of just a little more memory storage space.

Nesting loops can go well beyond the limit of two nests. Loops can be nested within nested loops within nested loops for as deep as you can keep them in order. Note that the FOR-NEXT pair must always be entirely contained within the last FOR-NEXT pair, otherwise you will get an error message. That is why the indentation of FOR-NEXT pairs for each successive pair makes error checking a lot easier.

SUBROUTINES

A small program designed to do a specialized calculation that may be needed fairly often is called a subroutine. For example, it is frequently necessary to test whether a number is positive, zero, or negative. In a checkbook program it could be terribly important to know if the balance is negative. Perhaps the first time you wrote the program you set it up out of the way at the end of your memory in a sequence that went like this:

```
5090 REMARK THIS SUB TELLS IF SIGN IS +, 0, OR −
5100 REMARK THE ROUTINE CHECKS VARIABLE X
5110 IF X > 0 THEN 5140
5120 IF X = 0 THEN 5160
5130 IF X < 0 THEN 5180
5140 PRINT "THE BALANCE IS POSITIVE!"
5150 RETURN
5160 PRINT "THE BALANCE IS ZERO!"
5170 RETURN
5180 PRINT "THE BALANCE IS NEGATIVE!"
5190 RETURN
```

Now anytime in your checkbook program that you want a printout of the state of your balance variable X, you insert the statement:

```
560 GOSUB 5090
```

When the computer gets to line 560 it will jump to 5090 just as it would with a straight GOTO statement, but it will keep track of 560 as the jumping-off place. It steps down through the subroutine, and when the proper PRINT statement has been output the subroutine signals RETURN. The program hops back to the next line after 560 and continues on.

This gives you the opportunity to custom write your own subroutines. A sign subroutine like this one may be used not only in a checkbook program but in an inventory of your pantry shelves.

Different "sizes" of BASIC offer more or fewer subroutines and commands. You can get a "Tiny" BASIC that will fit in 2K of random-access memory—which means you would need another couple of K for working programs. The standard BASIC usually fits in 8K. "Extended" BASIC usually requires 12K plus what you will want for programming. That range is enormous—from 2K to 12K—yet it is very convenient if you can write:

    80 T = SGN(X)

and automatically have T equal +1, 0, or −1 if X is positive, zero, or negative. Some trigonometric functions, logarithms, and so on are included in the smaller forms of BASIC and can be called up with a single statement. Others cannot and, for example, the square root function usually does not appear in a smaller BASIC. Instruction books and magazine articles list subroutines for programs which the user can write into his memory. The square-root subroutine will calculate the square root and even produce an appropriate error message if one is called for:

CAN'T CALCULATE ROOT OF A NEGATIVE NUMBER

if that is the case. The actual sequence of calculations used to figure the square root is called an "algorithm," and programmers can sometimes be overheard arguing about the relative speed or accuracy or elegance of a particular algorithm. One square-root algorithm starts with an approximation of the square root at half the given number and then calculates a series of closer approximations in a short loop until it is satisfied with the result which then returns to the main program.

DATA INPUT

We saw earlier that one way to get a number into the computer is to have the computer ask for it with a statement of the form:

    50 INPUT A

This is OK if only one or two numbers are involved. But if you have a whole series of numbers to be included, such as all your laundry bills for a year or every check you wrote last month, you would soon get tired of having the computer ask for the numbers one at a time. Instead you can put all the check values on a single line following a DATA statement. It would look like this:

850 DATA 24.50, 18.60, 36.14, 112.89, 99.95, 249.60

and so on. When you need more than one line for the data, you just put another DATA statement after the first. When you are ready in the program to input this data you call it out with a READ statement:

990 READ C

which tells the computer to take the first value from the DATA line wherever it may be. The DATA statement can be put at the very end of the program, at the beginning, or in the middle. It doesn't matter. The READ statement starts by calling up the first value it finds in the DATA line. If the READ statement is in a loop, it will call up the second value the second time around the loop and so on through all the loop circuits. You can write a little loop to read all the data:

```
990 FOR A = 1 TO 6
1000 READ C(A)
1010 NEXT A
```

Another way to input the data is to have the READ statement ask for more than one.

990 READ A, B, C, D, E, F

will assign the data values listed above to each of the variables A through F.

DATA-READ statements are a little tricky. Like the FOR-NEXT statements, they only work in pairs. If you ask for more READ variables than there are data, you will get an error message:

OUT OF DATA AT 1000

and the program will stop running. If you have typed in more data than the READ asks for, the overflow will be ignored.

If you have to read the same list of data into the program more than once, you can save the trouble of rewriting it by adding a RESTORE statement somewhere after the last READ. Think of the computer as having a pointer moving along the DATA line at each READ instruction. If the data are on more than one line, the pointer goes to the start of the second line immediately after the first line of data has been exhausted. The RESTORE statement snaps the point back to the first item in the first DATA statement.

DATA-READ statements are not my favorites in programming. For some reason it seems like a clumsy method of handling data, and it is difficult to keep track of. But it is the best we have.

RANDOM NUMBERS

One interesting subroutine which even the smallest version of BASIC will include is a random number generator. You need this for games of chance and for many other similar probability calculations. Different computers use slightly different grammar and vocabulary. The simplest is one in which you type:

    60 LET Y = RND(10)

to produce a value for Y that is any integer (whole number) between 1 and 10. The odds are equal for all the numbers so that 1 will come up 10% of the time as will 2, 3, 4, and so on. You may also type:

    60 LET Y = RND(0)

in which case Y will be any decimal fraction between 0 and 1. If you were programming a dice game, for example, and wanted the numbers to come up in their proper odds relationships for the throws between 2 and 12, you could have the computer pick a random number between 1 and 36:

```
60 LET Y = RND(36)
```

Later in your program you would assign values as follows:

IF Y IS	DICE SHOW
1	2
2	12
3–4	3
5–6	11
7–9	4
10–12	10
13–16	5
17–20	9
21–25	6
26–30	8
31–36	7

In this table there are two ways to make a 3, three ways to make a 4 or a 10, seven ways to make a 7, and thirty-six possible throws in all.

A simpler program method would duplicate the actual dice throw:

```
60 LET A = RND(6)
70 LET B = RND(6)
80 LET C = A + B
```

Now the odds are automatically taken care of, and the value of C is the dice throw in each instance.

Random numbers as generated in a computer are not really random in the sense that they are newly created each time you call for one. Odd as it may seem, there are such things as lists of random numbers—a list of decimal fractions between 0 and

1. When you call for a random number the computer goes to its list and pulls off the first value. The second time you call for a random number it goes back to the list and pulls off the second value. To find a random integer between 1 and 6 it just multiplies the value it finds by 6. It then rounds the number up—any number between 0 and 1 it calls 1, any number between 1 and 2 it calls 2, and so forth.

There is nothing wrong with this system except that each time you run the program it produces the same sequence of dice throws. That is an advantage when you are troubleshooting a program because you know what the values will be after each throw of the dice. It is a distinct problem when you are playing a real game. In that case you would randomize the start of the random number sequence—in effect you create a random selection of a random number, and that makes the odds of hitting the same sequence practically infinitesimal.

GRAPHICS

Most personal computers have facilities for creating graphic displays on their screens. Patterns like those you see in television commercials are often created this way. Lines and areas are white or dark. They grow or shrink, curve and twist in many wonderful ways—and you do this with programs.

The screen is divided into a grid pattern—say 128 by 48 rectangles addressed in X and Y coordinates from the top left corner of the screen. You can light up any particular rectangle with the statement:

    150 SET (X,Y)

and you turn it off by the statement:

    160 RESET (X,Y)

X and Y can be defined by an equation within a loop which recalculates their values after each cycle of the loop. With a little imagination and considerable programming you can create all sorts of displays, both fixed and moving. Pictures can be wiped on and off, lines drawn in endlessly repeating patterns, and so on. Some fairly sophisticated programming ability is required for graphics. Preprogrammed graphics are also available, and there are a couple of hobby computer interfaces with joystick controls that do all the programming chores—but more about that in the next chapter.

9

APPLICATIONS NOW

Have you ever wondered how television got started? I always imagine four or five high-pressure businessmen sitting around a big conference table and one of them looking up and saying, "Whaddaya say we start television?"

"Sure," says one of the others. "How?"

They need television sets manufactured, delivered, and sold at reasonable prices and in large quantities. They need to build transmitters, towers, and networks so that broadcasts can cover the entire country. They need writers and artists to prepare the material that will be televised. They need announcers and newscasters and entertainers. It is an industry that simply can't be started in a small way. Everything is needed at once—you can't sell sets without programs being transmitted; you can't afford to build transmitters unless you have advertisers; you can't get advertisers unless you have a lot of viewers out there watching; you can't get viewers unless you sell sets. It's the old chicken and egg conundrum. Which comes first? The answer: Everything.

So it is with home computers. If thousands of us are going to buy computers for our homes we need programs. It's a little easier than television because people can write their own programs. However, the people who can do this probably have hobby computers and will want more expensive equipment than the average consumer is willing to pay for. Currently the manufacturers of home computers are well ahead of the program writers. Complete, self-contained, and operable computers are on the market for less than $600, a sum which is within the means of many American families. There are no more than a few dozen programs available on tape right now, but there are hundreds in written form. They are in books, magazine articles, or are being exchanged at computer stores and clubs. Publishers will soon offer programs in any form you want—tape, disk, or printed. Here and in the next chapters we'll be looking at the kinds of programs available now and those that will be available in the near future.

Compatibility of equipment and programs is always a problem in an industry changing as rapidly as this one, but it isn't as troublesome as it might be. The home computer market was attacked from two directions by two different groups of manufacturers. The first were the video game manufacturers who started by hooking a few integrated circuits to a couple of knobs and wiring in a video modulator so that the unit could be connected to the antenna terminals of an ordinary television set. The success of these games has been so remarkable and the demand for even more challenging and complex games so strong that the manufacturers were forced to use a general purpose central processing unit. With the addition of read-only and random-access memory the video game became a true computer with different games entered by the loading of plug-in read-only memory boards. The trouble is that the plug-in boards or magnetic recordings from one company are not interchangeable with other manufacturers' equipment.

About the same time, large business computer designers

saw the potential of a computer in every home. They had already scaled down the million-dollar monsters to thousand-dollar units for small businesses. It was a logical step to redesign and reprice these units for the enormous home market. The computer manufacturers have pretty much standardized the language of the programs—BASIC—and the form—either cassette tape or floppy disk.

These manufacturers meet in the marketplace today in direct head-to-head competition between groups and, of course, within groups, with excellent equipment that requires two or more different forms of programming—some with standard audio cassettes, some with special cassettes, some with plug-in programmed read-only memory. At this point in time the flexibility and economy of the cassettes seem to have all the advantages—at least until disk drive prices come down a little more.

In any case the computer manufacturers and other specialized publishing companies are preparing all kinds of wonderful programs for us. It is a little easier to get some sense of what is available if we categorize the types of programs. There are a handful of major categories, and we will review them in order of popularity.

GAMES

There are literally hundreds of games programmed for play on a home computer. All are in BASIC, but since there may be minor differences in the statements and syntax, make sure the one you get is compatible with your computer or that you know the differences so that appropriate changes can be made. Tape and disk are fairly expensive, and typing a long program line by line can be a tedious and error-prone exercise. However, many of the published games are fewer than twenty lines long and can be great fun for you or your children.

The simplest are number or letter guessing games. The computer picks a number from 1 to 100 and you have to find it. Clues differ depending on the game. In one you are told you are too high or too low. In another you try to trap the number between the two selected numbers.

Word guessing games are a little more complicated because they require a dictionary of selections to be put in by the programmer. The most familiar of these is *Hangman* which is exactly like the game schoolchildren play with paper and pencil. The computer selects a word at random and prints an underline for each letter in the word. You guess the letters one at a time. If the letter you guess is in the word, the computer prints it in its proper place, leaving underlines for the others. If the letter you choose is not in the word, the computer starts to draw a picture of a hanging man. If you miss too often, the picture is completed and you lose the game.

This can be a difficult game even for adults if the dictionary includes words with unusual combinations of letters. A surefire problem word is one like *taxi*—particularly in those versions of the game in which the number of guesses is limited to the number of letters in the word.

Synonym is a game that presents you with a word and asks for a synonym. The computer has a dictionary of words and their synonyms and simply checks to see if your answer is in its list. *Scrambled Word* takes the letters in a word from its dictionary and switches them around before printing them on the screen. You set a time limit for yourself, and if you can type the correct word before the time limit is up, you score 1, if not you score 0. The computer will figure your average time to unscramble or total the scores at the end of ten words.

Number and word guessing games are very simple programs for the computer. The random number generator selects the number, and IF-THEN statements give the conditional jump, depending on your guess, which takes the player to the proper clues and eventually to the "RIGHT!" ending. Word-guessing games require a dictionary of words in DATA statements, which means the programmer can't really play because he knows what he put in the dictionary.

Numbers in piles make for a set of games that are somewhat more complicated. *Nim* is a very old Chinese game. In the original version there are three piles of stones or chips with four, five, and six chips. Each player gets a turn and removes at least one and as many as all the chips in any one pile. In one version the object of the game is to get the last chip. In another version the object is to force the opposing player to take the last chip. It is a real challenge to discover the strategy to win this game. There is one, and it is mathematically based. It is a binary computation, but not one that you would derive intuitively; however, it can be deduced after practice with different combinations. The strategy is easily programmed and permits a much broader game to be set up. You can vary the number of chips in each pile at the start and add to the number of piles if you like. This makes the game much harder for humans but no more complex for the computer.

Other number pile games are simpler. In one you start with 23 matches in the pile. On each turn either you or the computer may take from 1 to 3 matches out of the pile. The one who takes the last match loses. In *Even*, an odd number of matches are in the pile. On each turn you take from 1 to 4 matches. When all the matches have been removed the player who has collected an even number wins.

After a few tries at number piles the matrix and grid games offer a pleasant visual relief. These are usually played on a 10 by 10 grid identified by X and Y coordinates. You are trying to find the *Hurkle, Mugwump,* or *Snark* (depending on the rules) which is hiding at some point on the grid. The computer places the Snark at, say, point 5,3. That means he is at the intersection of column 5 and row 3. You are given an opportunity to guess an intersection which you identify by its coordinates. Then the computer gives you a clue as to the Snark location relative to your guess. The clue may be a direction ("NO HIT, GO NORTHEAST") or a distance ("YOU ARE 3.3 UNITS AWAY FROM THE HURKLE"), or you choose location and a radius, and the computer will tell you whether the Snark is inside or outside the circle drawn with its center at the location and with the given radius.

Let's play this game once so you get the idea. In the normal computer run the grid pattern is only drawn once, and the rest of the game is played as printed out below this grid.

WANT THE RULES? YES

A SNARK IS HIDING IN A 10 BY 10 GRID LIKE THIS ONE:

```
Y
9   .   .   .   .   .   .   .   .   .   .
8   .   .   .   .   .   .   .   .   .   .
7   .   .   .   .   .   .   .   .   .   .
6   .   .   .   .   .   .   .   .   .   .
5   .   .   .   .   .   .   .   .   .   .
4   .   .   .   .   .   .   .   .   .   .
3   .   .   .   .   .   .   .   .   .   .
2   .   .   .   .   .   .   .   .   .   .
1   .   .   .   .   .   .   .   .   .   .
0   .   .   .   .   .   .   .   .   .   .
    0   1   2   3   4   5   6   7   8   9   X
```

TRY TO CATCH HIM. HERE IS HOW. WHEN I ASK, YOU TYPE THE X,Y COORDINATES OF A GRIDPOINT AND PRESS RETURN. WHEN I ASK FOR "RADIUS" YOU TYPE THE RADIUS OF A CIRCLE CENTERED ON YOUR CHOSEN GRIDPOINT. I WILL THEN TELL YOU WHETHER THE SNARK IS INSIDE OR OUTSIDE YOUR CIRCLE.

OK. THE SNARK IS HIDING. START GUESSING.

COORDINATES?4,4
RADIUS?3
SNARK IS OUTSIDE YOUR CIRCLE

COORDINATES?7,7
RADIUS?2
SNARK IS INSIDE YOUR CIRCLE

```
COORDINATES?7,7
RADIUS?1
SNARK IS INSIDE YOUR CIRCLE

COORDINATES?7,8
RADIUS?0
SNARK IS OUTSIDE YOUR CIRCLE

COORDINATES?8,7
RADIUS?0

YOU CAUGHT HIM IN 5 GUESSES!!!!
VERY GOOD!

WANT TO PLAY AGAIN?NO

READY
```

A logical extension of matrix games are board games. These are played on a field like an 8 by 8 checkerboard. In *Queen* the only piece on the board is a chess queen which can move left, down, or diagonally down to the left for as many spaces as you like. The queen starts in the upper right corner and you get the first move. The object is to place the queen in the lower left corner. The computer can be beaten once you learn the sequence of safe positions in which to put the queen.

Much more difficult is a game called *1Check* which has 48 checkers (zeros) placed in the two outside rows of the checkerboard:

```
0   0   0   0   0   0   0   0
0   0   0   0   0   0   0   0
0   0   -   -   -   -   0   0
0   0   -   -   -   -   0   0
0   0   -   -   -   -   0   0
0   0   -   -   -   -   0   0
0   0   0   0   0   0   0   0
0   0   0   0   0   0   0   0
```

The object is to remove as many checkers as possible by diagonal jumps as in standard checkers. It is easy to remove 30 to

39 checkers, a challenge to get to 44, and a substantial feat to get 45 to 47.

There is a standard checker game which you can play, but the program that will fit in a small computer cannot accept multiple jumps, which limits the challenge somewhat.

I think the best of the board games are *Gomoku* and *Qubic*. *Gomoku* is a traditional Japanese game played on a 19 by 19 board. Small computers can't handle a board of that size, so they play on a 10 by 10 board. Each player takes a turn putting his piece (a 0 or an X) on the squares of the board. You identify the location with the usual X,Y coordinates. The object is to get five pieces in a straight line either horizontally, vertically, or diagonally. The computer has a nice strategy which is not too hard to beat once you get the feel of the game.

Qubic is three-dimensional tic-tac-toe played in a 4 by 4 by 4 cube. It is simplest to draw the four planes separately.

```
                          Columns
            1 2 3 4   1 2 3 4   1 2 3 4   1 2 3 4
    R  1    . . . .   . . . .   . . . .   . . . .
    o  2    . . . .   . . . .   . . . .   . . . .
    w  3    . . . .   . . . .   . . . .   . . . .
    s  4    . . . .   . . . .   . . . .   . . . .
            Level 1   Level 2   Level 3   Level 4
```

You identify a point in the cube with three coordinates—level, row, and column—and alternate turns with the computer in an attempt to get possession of four points in a straight line. There are 76 possible straight lines, and the more elaborate *Qubic* programs permit you to set a level of difficulty with the computer as opponent.

At its lowest level the computer offensive strategy picks a row at random and continues to play in that row until blocked. On the defensive it checks all possible combinations to see if you have three points in a row and will make the stopping play if you do.

At higher levels the computer will pick two intersecting rows, fill two squares in each row, and then play the intersection to get two three-in-a-row combinations simultaneously. On the defensive it will check to see if you have the potential to make two three-in-a-row combinations and play the blocking move if you do. *Qubic* is a good exercise of your ability to visualize if you dare to play without paper or pencil but a tough game even with these props.

Computer games of logic are, with very few exceptions, based on puzzles that have entertained people for hundreds of years. The *Tower of Hanoi* is, for example, an old Middle Eastern game often reproduced in modern form as a wood or plastic puzzle. It has three spikes with seven holed disks whose diameters are graduated from smallest to largest.

```
      X   |  X               |                  |
     XX   |  XX              |                  |
    XXX   |  XXX             |                  |
   XXXX   |  XXXX            |                  |
  XXXXX   |  XXXXX           |                  |
 XXXXXX   |  XXXXXX          |                  |
XXXXXXX   |  XXXXXXX         |                  |
```

The trick is to transfer all the disks from the left tower to the right one. However, only one disk may be moved at each step, and you must never put a larger disk on top of a smaller one. Since there is a pattern of moves that quickly develops and repeats, it soon becomes a practiced routine and a bore.

Flipflop seems like a very simple puzzle at first. You start with a row of Xs each identified by a number, like this:

```
X   X   X   X   X   X   X   X   X   X
1   2   3   4   5   6   7   8   9   10
```

The object is to get all the Xs changed to 0s. By typing a number corresponding to one of the Xs you change that X to a 0 or, if it is a 0, it will change back to an X. The problem is that some of the choices will change more than one letter, so there is some backsliding when a 0 goes back to being an X.

Reverse is a straight logical challenge though the starting position may make some examples much more difficult than others. You are given a randomly selected set of nine numbers in a row and the object is to get them into numerical sequence in as few moves as possible. You may reverse any number starting from the left end. For example, if the given list is:

2   3   4   5   6   1   7   8   9

and you reverse five you get

6   5   4   3   2   1   7   8   9

and now you reverse six and get

1   2   3   4   5   6   7   8   9

Another logic game is a more complex form of the popular *Mastermind* which recently swept the market. In the computer it is variously called *Bulcow* or *Moo*. The computer selects a four-digit number. No two digits are alike. You must guess the selected number based on clues given after each guess. If the selected digit is correct and in the right place, you are given a BULL. If the selected digit is correct but in the wrong place, you are given a COW. If you have neither the right digit nor the right place you get no clues. Here is a sample game:

THE NUMBER IS SELECTED. WHAT IS YOUR GUESS? 1234

NO CLUES.

WHAT IS YOUR GUESS? 5678

COW COW   (You got two right numbers.)

YOUR GUESS? 5789

COW COW COW   (Added one with the 9.)

YOUR GUESS? 5890

BULL BULL COW   (The 0 may be right, 5 or 8 wrong.)

YOUR GUESS? 7890

BULL BULL COW COW   (Numbers all right;
                                         two in wrong places.)

YOUR GUESS? 9870
BULL BULL BULL BULL

There is an element of luck but strong logic speeds the solution dramatically.

Gambling games are easy to program and can be great fun. *One-Armed Bandit, Dice,* and *Blackjack* programs will allocate you a certain amount of money which you can lose entirely or run up to thousands, depending on your strategy and luck. If you are practicing in anticipation of a trip to Las Vegas, the computer will give you the perfect "house" to play against, and it is a painless lesson if you lose.

Sports are simulated in a number of games—bowling, boxing, football, golf, baseball, and even skiing and auto racing. You control certain variables of play, and the computer randomizes among the outcomes play by play, inning by inning, or road section by road section to the conclusion of the game. Most often you score against time or some maximum achievable score.

So far, all the games I have described are essentially mechanized versions of older games or puzzles. We are now just beginning to see a few game programs that tax the power of the computer. Such is *Startrek*—one of the two most popular games now played on computers. There are several dozen variations, but the essential plot is the same. You are the captain of the Starship *Enterprise.* Your mission is to find and destroy enemy Klingon cruisers (there may be dozens) with torpedos or phaser energy beams. Your ship is protected by energy shields, and periodically you must recharge your energy cells at starbases strategically located in space. You must navigate, scan near and far space quadrants to locate the enemy. You aim and fire your weapons and must determine how much energy to put into the defensive screens. As in most good games, this one requires some study to understand all the rules and the way to write choices. However, once they are learned, you will enjoy an exciting and continually interesting game.

Kingdom is a game of similar complexity. You are the king of a small country and must decide how much land to put under cultivation in order to feed your people. Grain planted is not available for food, of course, and the amount of grain that will grow depends on weather, disease, and the rapacious intentions of neighboring countries. Luck and disaster hang around every turn, and if your people starve you may be assassinated or jailed. This game and *Stock Market* are called simulation games and have great value in teaching social science and business in schools. In *Stock Market* you are given $10,000 to buy and sell one or more of five listed stocks. The stock prices change randomly after every day's trading, at which time a table is printed listing the stocks, their prices, and your position in each. Your total assets in stock and cash are also listed. You may buy or sell as many shares as your financial resources permit. A small brokerage fee is charged for every transaction. You play as long as you like and watch your estate grow or disappear.

Lem has that same teaching potential, though it is essentially mathematical in nature. You are the pilot of the lunar landing module which, at the start of play, is 500 feet above the surface of the moon and falling at a speed of 50 feet per second. You have 120 units of fuel in your tanks and you must set the burn rate of the retro rockets to slow the speed of descent to less than 5 feet per second to make a safe landing. It takes a minimum burn rate of 5 units of fuel per second to hold the descent speed unchanged against the moon's gravitational attraction. A smaller burn rate will permit the descent speed to increase. Here is a sample run:

STARTING HEIGHT: 500 FT
STARTING SPEED: 50 FT/SEC
FUEL SUPPLY: 120 UNITS
MAXIMUM BURN: 30 UNITS/SEC
BURN TO CANCEL GRAVITY OF MOON: 5 UNITS/SEC

CRASH TIME: 7.32051 SEC
CRASH SPEED: 86.6025 FT/SEC

BURN	TIME	HEIGHT	SPEED	FUEL
	0	500	50	120
? 0				
	1	447.5	55	120
? 0				
	2	390	60	120
? 0				
	3	327.5	65	120
? 10				
	4	265	60	110
? 20				
	5	212.5	45	90
? 15				
	6	172.5	35	75
? 10				
	7	140	30	65
? 10				
	8	112.5	25	55
? 10				
	9	90	20	45
? 10				
	10	72.5	15	35
? 5				
	11	57.5	15	30
? 5				
	12	42.5	15	25

BURN	TIME	HEIGHT	SPEED	FUEL
? 5				
	13	27.5	15	20
? 10				
	14	15	10	10
? 10				
	15	7.5	5	OUT OF FUEL. FREE FALL STARTS NOW.
0				
	16	0	10	0

CLOSE DOESN'T COUNT.

We did pretty well on this trial. Sixteen seconds after the start of the fall we hit the ground (height 0) with empty fuel tanks. The only problem is that our speed of descent was 10 feet per second, which is approximately 15 miles per hour and twice the maximum speed allowed. The program has a number of sarcastic lines to offer when you run out of fuel and are still well above the surface or when you hit so hard that you seem to be trying to dig your way underground. Here's a perfect landing:

BURN	TIME	HEIGHT	SPEED	FUEL
	0	500	50	120
? 0				
	1	447.5	55	120
? 0				
	2	390	60	120
? 0				
	3	327.5	65	120
? 0				
	4	260	70	120
? 0				
	5	187.5	75	120

BURN	TIME	HEIGHT	SPEED	FUEL
? 20				
	6	120	60	100
? 20				
	7	67.5	45	80
? 20				
	8	30	30	60
? 20				
	9	7.5	15	40
? 20				
	10	0	0	20

OUTASIGHT.

You can make the situation more complicated by changing the starting height and speed as well as the force of gravity (you land on Earth instead of the moon). It's a good challenge and remarkably interesting, considering the entire output is in the form of a table of numbers.

Video games are still available as separate devices that attach to a television set, but you can also get programs that work in the same way on your home computer. *Tennis, Hockey,* and *Soccer* games have one or more bars of light representing your "men" and others representing your opponent's. A smaller spot bounces back and forth across the screen and your object is, usually, to hit the spot so that it goes past your opponent. A second generation of such video games includes mazes and simulations of tanks, airplanes, or Western-style gunslingers with opposing players steering, aiming, and shooting. These games are too familiar to warrant any more space in this book.

CREATIVE GRAPHICS

At first it may be strange to think of the computer as an art form, but it is, no matter how you interpret the expression. As we saw in the chapter on programming, it is possible to write programs that paint light on the screen and make it change with time. Your most fanciful visions are within reach—I have seen circles grow, dance, and fade, points of light trace weird and repetitive designs, objects seem to twist and turn in space and then change into things too strange to describe.

The development of the computer as an artistic medium is as genuinely original as was the invention of the camera. There are techniques to learn—in this case a language and mathematics of programming—few home computers offer the freedom of color choice. But the added dimension of time makes the graphics a dynamic rather than static creation. For that reason computer art is more like film or television than traditional painting or graphics.

The computer can plot graphs of all kinds from simple X-Y graphs to bar charts and pie diagrams. Would you like to graph your income over the years, a child's growth, or the floor plan of your home as it is and might be? All are easily programmed and drawn on the screen and may be stored for repeated viewing any time.

Programs are available that will print out a banner headline, in poster form, of any message you write. The characters of the poster are made of typewriter letters or symbols—whatever is available on your keyboard.

Here is a sample:

```
LLLL                     OOOOOOOOOOOOOO    VVVV              VVVV EEEEEEEEEEEEEEEEEE
LLLL                    OOOOOOOOOOOOOOOOO   VVVV             VVVV  EEEEEEEEEEEEEEEEEE
LLLL                   OOOOOOOOOOOOOOOOOOO  VVVV            VVVV   EEEEEEEEEEEEEEEEEE
LLLL            OOOO                 OOOO   VVVV           VVVV    EEEE
LLLL           OOOO                   OOOO   VVVV         VVVV     EEEE
LLLL           OOOO                   OOOO    VVVV       VVVV      EEEE
LLLL           OOOO                   OOOO     VVVV     VVVV       EEEEEEEEEEEE
LLLL           OOOO                   OOOO      VVVV   VVVV        EEEEEEEEEEEE
LLLL           OOOO                   OOOO       VVVV VVVV         EEEEEEEEEEEE
LLLL           OOOO                   OOOO        VVV VVV          EEEE
LLLL           OOOO                   OOOO         VVVVVVV         EEEE
LLLL            OOOO                 OOOO           VVV VVV        EEEE
LLLLLLLLLLLLLLLLLLLLLL  OOOOOOOOOOOOOOOOO           VVVVV          EEEEEEEEEEEEEEEEEE
LLLLLLLLLLLLLLLLLLLLLL   OOOOOOOOOOOOOOO             VVV           EEEEEEEEEEEEEEEEEE
LLLLLLLLLLLLLLLLLLLLLL    OOOOOOOOOOOOO               VV           EEEEEEEEEEEEEEEEEE
```

This looks pretty good on the screen but even better if you can get it typed out on a printer.

One of the more interesting graphic programs is a computerization of a game called *Life*. *Life* was invented by an Englishman named John Conway and published in *Scientific American* in 1970. It works like this: Imagine an infinite checkerboard with squares going north, south, east, and west. You place a small number of counters (checkers) on the board in any pattern you choose. The counters reproduce, survive, or die out in each generation according to three rules:

1. A counter with four or more neighbors (other counters in adjacent squares) dies (is removed) from overpopulation. A counter with one neighbor or none dies from isolation.

2. A counter with two or three neighbors survives to the next generation.

3. An empty cell which has three neighbors exactly is a birth cell. A counter is placed there for the next generation.

All births and deaths occur simultaneously at the end of each generation. The game, if it is a game, is to watch the changing generations as they grow or decline from different source patterns. Some patterns eventually stabilize into what Conway calls "still lifes," which do not change anymore or which oscillate between two symmetrical patterns. Here are two samples; the first is called "Fuze":

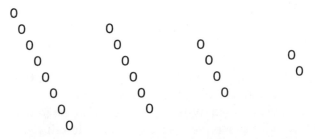

Generation 1 Generation 2 Generation 3 Generation 4 Generation 5

This one is called "Spaceship and Planet":

```
0  0         0  0          0  0          0  0
0  0         0  0          0  0          0  0
   0
      0             0
0  0  0                 0                 0
             0  0  0                 0                 0
                          0  0  0                 0
                                            0  0  0
```

Generation 1   Generation 5   Generation 9   Generation 13

Note that the Spaceship moves away from the Planet but not in succeeding generations. The Spaceship goes through a series of other changes before it reappears in its original form but in a new location.

EDUCATIONAL PROGRAMS

The most promising area for programming and one of the slowest to develop is education and instruction. Some years ago, when large computers first became available to scientists, a few psychologists experimented with a teaching method that reduced a course of study into small, easily digested capsules. Each "bite" was given to the student and then followed by a question or two which would determine whether the student had understood the information. This immediate feedback was called "reinforcement" and was thought to be critically important to the successful learner. The method was a natural for the computer, and since the first attempts were written in program form, they were called "programmed learning." Despite initial success the method was received with considerable criticism from teachers—they found their students spending more time at the computer terminal than in the classroom—who were reluctant to revise their thinking to accommodate the demands of computer programming.

Today there are only a few such programs available, though more will be coming soon (see the next chapter). In the meantime programs where the computer functions as a drill instructor are being used for grade school children in subjects like arithmetic and spelling.

A computer will teach addition, subtraction, multiplication, and division with infinite patience for the necessary repetition. The program presents a problem:

```
6 + 5 = ?
```

The student types the answer:

```
6 + 5 = ?11
RIGHT!
8 + 3 = ?12
NOT QUITE. TRY AGAIN?11
RIGHT!
```

and so on. Usually the program will present ten problems and keep score, then give the student an accounting. If the scores are uniformly good, the program will step up to a more difficult level.

Spelling works in a slightly different way. As in an ordinary spelling book the program starts with a vocabulary of words which are grouped from easiest to hardest. The program picks a word at random from a designated group and displays it on the screen for a very limited period of time—perhaps a second. The student must then retype the word. It is amazing that this approach teaches so effectively. The simple exercise of having to remember the word and type it engraves it on the memory.

The display is shown for too short a time to permit unthinking copying of the word, and I have seen well-read English teachers misspell unfamiliar words as often as fourth-grade students misspell words unfamiliar to them.

KITCHEN RECIPES

When they were introducing the first generation of home computers, manufacturers made much of the kitchen programs that were included with the demonstration tapes. These early programs included a library of recipes plus ratio adjustments of recipe measures to change for the number of people who might be served. You call for a recipe for stew, for example, that would normally serve four people. Then you indicate that the recipe needs to be expanded to feed twelve. The computer multiplies all measures by three and prints out a new recipe.

Even simpler for the computer is a straight weights-and-measures converter. The program has stored all the usual measures—teaspoonsful, tablespoonsful, cups and liquid ounces, pounds, feet, and all their metric equivalents like cubic centimeters, grams, meters, and liters.

When you enter one teaspoonful for a recipe and want it expanded for a larger dinner party, the computer automatically multiplies by the proper number and shifts to the new measure if that is indicated. Three cups of milk, for example, when multiplied by four become twelve cups or three quarts.

The computer as recipe file has distinct disadvantages. Each recipe has to be retyped entirely and, for a full cookbook, that can be something of a chore. Also, if you don't remember each recipe name in the file, you will spend a lot of time searching through the recipes to find the one you want.

A second method would leave the printed version of the recipe in its original form—either an entry in a cookbook, a page from a magazine, or scrawled on the back of an envelope. You store the recipes on your bookshelf or in a file folder. The only important change you have to make to the recipe is the addition of an identifying number of some kind—perhaps a chronological list that starts with number 1 and just keeps growing with each new recipe. As each recipe is added to your file you type into the computer the number, the name, the location, and any other descriptive words that might be appropriate. You might use the course it is usually served for (appetizer, soup, main course, dessert); the main ingredient (beef, pork, fish, cheese); the method of cooking (casserole, roast, boil); cuisine (French, American, Oriental); or suitability for certain meals (large dinner party, dinner for two, brunch, luncheon).

Now you have a set of descriptive words that categorize each recipe in a number of different ways. You use the logical power of the computer to do the selection. For example, you might decide you want a main course for an elegant dinner party for your boss. You decide it must be a roast. You type:

SELECT MAIN COURSE AND ROAST

The "and" in this example is used in its strict logical sense, which means: Select those recipes which are identified as main courses but which are also described as roasts. The computer starts a list of "sets" which are groups of recipes:

SET	DESCRIPTOR	ITEMS
1	MAIN COURSE	758
2	ROAST	353
3	1 AND 2	150

This indicates that you have 758 main courses in your file, 353 roast dishes, and 150 roast main courses. You don't want to look at a list of 150 recipe names, so you decide to make a new limitation on the list:

SELECT 3 AND FOWL

SET	DESCRIPTOR	ITEMS
1	MAIN COURSE	758
2	ROAST	353
3	1 AND 2	150
4	FOWL	280
5	3 AND 4	10

This tells you that the number of main course fowl roasts is 10. That's more like it. You now want a printout of the 10 items so you type:

LIST SET 5

and the names of the 10 recipes are listed out with the identifying number for each and some indication of location:

NAME	NUMBER	LOCATION
CHICKEN WITH TARRAGON	46	FILE FOLDER
CHICKEN WITH RICE	85	COOKBOOK NO. 5
DUCK WITH ORANGE SAUCE	145	COOKBOOK NO. 9

and so on.

INDEXES AND INFORMATION RETRIEVAL

Information retrieval programs of this kind work as well for a Christmas list, a phone number list, an appointment calendar, or any other set of data which you want to store as "records" in a file and that are called out with a set of category words called "descriptors." You choose your descriptors with care to suit your own thinking or memory patterns. You may want to keep a separate list of the descriptors used for each file to jog your memory when you plan to search the file.

An appointment calendar is an even more elementary form of retrieval program because the descriptor is always the date, and you add items or records to the file by date and time. When you want to call up a particular day's appointments the computer searches through its memory for all items identified with the given date. It then sorts them according to time and prints out the results in a neat table:

APPOINTMENT CALENDAR FOR JANUARY 8, 1980

TIME	DESCRIPTION
9:00	PHONE JOHN MALLOY
9:20	MEET WITH FRANCES PARK
10:45	HAIRCUT
12:00	LUNCH WITH FRED
3:30	VP MEETING—BOARDROOM
5:30	DINNER RESERVATION AT ITALIAN VILLA

and, of course, you can include whatever notes to yourself that seem appropriate. They will be printed out at the given time or at the end of the day's listing.

These sorting routines don't take much memory space, though the information itself may take a lot of tape. The sorting routine can be added to the start of every such cassette file. When loaded into random-access memory the sorting routine takes over the search and retrieve functions on the rest of the tape without putting the entire tape into electronic memory.

The retrieval program has many advantages for a phone number list as well. Each name and phone number is identified by descriptors that are useful to you in remembering. The words might be things like butcher, cleaner, roof repair, yardwork, antique store, plumber, summer 1977, green dress, brunette. The computer will search under these names as well as the actual name of the individual if you know it. You can also search by an identifying number if you include one or the date when the name had been added to the list. Thus you could have the computer print out the phone numbers of everyone added to the list during June 1975 or all the names that begin with F or all the names of brunettes wearing green dresses.

Obviously the Christmas list is exactly the same with the added possibility of keeping track of who got what Christmas card or present and when.

BUDGETING

Businesses have been using large accounting programs for many years to prepare corporate budgets, and it was easy to adapt them for personal use on small computers. Perhaps two dozen different categories of expenses are identified—mortgage/rent, food, clothing, insurance, utilities, taxes, and so on. You set a budget figure for each category for any time period that is convenient—say monthly. A budget list can then be printed out indicating the category, the monthly amount budgeted, and, at the bottom, the total you must earn to cover the expenses.

BUDGET STATEMENT

	MARCH		YEAR TO DATE	
CATEGORY	BUDGET	ACTUAL	BUDGET	ACTUAL
RENT	200	200.00	600	600.00
FOOD	120	92.65	360	335.14
CLOTHES	50	126.00	150	228.50
INSURANCE	25	50.00	75	50.00
UTILITIES	30	62.50	90	93.75
ENTERTAINMENT	100	125.00	300	265.00
TOTALS	525	656.15	1575	1572.39

If the budgeted total is larger than your income, you will either have to find some additional income or reduce the expenses. This becomes the budget for the coming year against which actual expenses will be measured. Suppose you enter at the end of March all of your March expenses, taken from your checkbook, as you have been doing for the last three months. Page 202 shows how a budget statement might look.

Businessmen use this sort of statement to analyze the condition of their companies and to see how they are actually doing compared to their expectations. The total tells you whether you are living within your income or not. A given expense item may go over or under your budget from month to month as extraordinary expenses hit your checkbook, but the accumulations in the year-to-date columns should tell you, after a few months, whether your budget was reasonable and if you have accumulated some extra savings to use for a vacation or, perhaps, a new computer.

Checkbook programs work like bank statements. The difference is that you can keep track of your balance throughout the month and rest assured your additions and subtractions are ac-

ITEM	AMOUNT	BALANCE
OPENING		323.44
RENT–HOUSE REALTY	125.00	198.44
CAR GAS—HH OIL CO.	16.80	181.64
CLOTHES–DEPT. STORE INC.	75.00	106.64
DEPOSIT	258.30	364.94
TELEPHONE	26.80	338.14
VACATION–AIRLINE	198.00	140.14
CHARGE ACCOUNT	130.00	10.14
DINNER–FRED RESTAURANT	18.60	− 8.46
OVERDRAFT CHARGE	1.00	− 9.46
DEPOSIT	258.30	248.84
CLOSING JANUARY 8, 1980		248.84

curate. You enter each check as it is written with date, payee, and amount. You enter each deposit by amount and date. The program will give a balance anytime. When the bank statement arrives each month, you add a note to tell the program that a check has cleared (been cashed by the payee) and then run a quick reconciliation between your program and the bank statement. A simple checkbook program might produce a listing like that on page 203.

The computer will not know the closing date unless it has a battery-operated clock built into its electronics, but it is easy enough to add the date when you call up the closing statement or when you do the accounting.

10

THE NEXT
FEW YEARS

Combine a cathode ray tube display with a keyboard and you
have a terminal—the main communications link between you
and the computer. Add an acoustic coupler, and you can communicate with other terminals or computers through telephone lines and at a distance. The effect is to give you access to
computers with much larger computational ability and, even
more important, with much larger memories.

In a good system the computer, whether in your home or in
a distant city, becomes "transparent." You don't see it and are
not aware of it as a separate entity. You deal with the information in the big data bases (jargon for masses of information
stored in computer memory) in an "interactive" way. That is,
you converse with the computer-as-librarian or the computer-
as-bank-teller or the computer-as-accountant in much the same
way you converse with their human counterparts.

The distinction between your home computer and the distant larger one or the computer in some other user's home
begins to blur. All interact in a vast computer network which

becomes larger than the sum of its parts. When we speak of what is possible in computers, it is this larger network we have to keep in mind.

You are not the sole user of the computer-at-a-distance. You share it with hundreds of others at the same time, perhaps within the same second. In "time-sharing," the computer steps from user to user in turn, devoting a few hundredths of a second to each. It moves so fast that each user is totally unaware of the other users unless specifically communicating with someone through the computer. Today there are several dozen computer companies whose only business is to make computer time available to subscribers. They offer hundreds of programs from games to business accounting, from statistical analysis to engineering design, which you may use as is or in conjunction with your own data.

There are even companies that provide a network of long-distance telephone lines all over the world. Thus a subscriber in Los Angeles or South Africa may use a computer in New Jersey at rates that are much lower than the normal long-distance telephone charges. You dial a local number in your city which hooks you into the network. You then ask for a particular computer and the network puts you through.

Time-sharing is not cheap today. Right now you can expect to pay a minimum of $10 an hour and often a lot more, depending on the particular programs being used. Add the network charges and few people can afford it just for entertainment. But as computers and terminals find their way into more and more homes the costs will drop dramatically.

Time-sharing is handled on a subscriber basis and works something like this: you dial a given telephone number. When it is answered (with a high-pitched squeal) you put the handset into the rubber cups of the acoustic coupler and touch the RETURN button on your keyboard. Immediately letters begin to appear on the screen:

HELLO. PLEASE SIGN ON.

You type an identification number for billing purposes:

SMITH101
PASSWORD?

It is asking for a password that will establish the security on the information you may be storing. Since many people use the same computer, some method of limiting the transfer of information from user to user is necessary. The best method devised so far is for users to choose their own passwords, which act as keys to their data files in the same way that a safety deposit key allows only the owner of a deposit box access to the vault. You may choose a password of up to 8 letters, numbers, or symbols on your keyboard. There are 52 uppercase and lowercase letters, 10 numbers, and about two dozen symbols. Therefore the number of possible combinations is 86 raised to the eighth power or 3 followed by 15 zeros—well beyond what anyone will ever guess unless you make it easy by picking your name or some other obvious choice. A password can be changed at any time. However you have to be careful not to forget it, or any information you have stored will be lost. So you type your password:

PICKLE

WELCOME TO COMPUTER WORLD. WE HAVE
THOUSANDS OF EXCITING THINGS FOR YOU TO
DO—GAMES, PUZZLES, INFORMATION, READING
AND REFERENCE MATERIAL, CURRENT NEWS. YOUR
INSTRUCTION BOOK AND CATALOG HAVE THE
CURRENT LIST. WOULD YOU LIKE TO SEE THE
GENERAL CATEGORIES OF MATERIAL NOW
AVAILABLE?

YES

GENERAL SUBJECT CATEGORIES:
1. EDUCATIONAL PROGRAMS
2. GAMES
3. HOUSEHOLD
4. LIBRARY REFERENCE
5. CURRENT EVENTS
6. SHOPPING
IF YOU WANT A MORE DETAILED LISTING OF
PROGRAMS IN ANY OF THE ABOVE CATEGORIES
JUST TYPE THE NUMBER OF THE LISTING. IF NOT,
CALL FOR THE SPECIFIC PROGRAM OF YOUR CHOICE
BY ITS NAME AS LISTED IN THE CATALOG.

You decide to see what is in the library reference list and
therefore type:

4

LIBRARY REFERENCE
WE HAVE MOST STANDARD REFERENCE BOOKS ON
FILE WHICH MAY BE CALLED UP ON YOUR SCREEN.
THESE INCLUDE:

ADVISOR FOR POISONS, STAINS AND OTHER HOUSEHOLD AIDS	ADV*
BIOGRAPHICAL REFERENCES	BIO*
DICTIONARIES—STANDARD, CROSSWORD, RHYMING	DICT*
ENCYCLOPEDIA	ENCY*
PERIODICAL INDEXES	PER*
READER'S ENCYCLOPEDIA	READ*
TRAVEL GUIDE	TRAV*

READY

The encyclopedia is larger than any you could afford to buy
and store in printed form. It is updated daily as is the periodi-
cal index and the other references. The encyclopedia includes
medical advice, legal advice, tax advice. If you want to find a
particular page or paragraph, the computer asks for a subject

word and displays the index entries around the chosen word, so you can pick the specific subject you want. There is a page reference which calls up the particular page or diagram. The computer will fill the screen of your terminal and then wait until you call for the next page, if there is one.

Some of the references are a little unusual. The crossword puzzle dictionary will list all five-letter words whose second letter is "d," or all seven-letter words ending in "stion." The purists will say this is cheating, but they don't have to use it if they don't want to.

The biographical references include all the "Who's Whos" in print referenced by name, profession, location of residence. The travel guide can be entered by location, type of accommodations, airfare, major activities.

Time-sharing offers a new dimension to the familiar library—a currency and completeness unknown anywhere today. It offers the possibility of direct communication between users, which we will be talking about later, and a much larger memory bank than will ever be available to the home computer.

So in all that follows let us take time-sharing as a given. The home computer has its own computing power, its own memory, its own files of information of concern to the owner. But via telephone lines or microwave antennas it can reach out to a much larger network of communication with other time-sharing computers, with other individual users, and possibly with special school or commercial computers for a thousand specialized applications.

APPLIANCE CONTROL

Let's start close to home. The home computer of the not-too-distant future will have plenty of input and output circuits for appliance control. It will have adequate memory and will run power-on for 24 hours a day to control the central heating system, the vacuum cleaner, drier, washing machine, microwave oven, room lights, stereo—and even permit the selection of music by mood or instrument as well as selection name.

Once voice recognition is programmed with reliability and economy we will have our computer answering the front door and letting friends in while keeping strangers out. It will be the ideal house sitter and burglar alarm. It will identify family sounds and movements throughout the house and sound an alarm when normal patterns are disturbed. When you are away on vacation the computer will program lights and sounds to simulate an occupied house. It will sense intrusions at door or windows and contact the local police. It will sense smoke or fire and call the local fire department as well as sound a loud alarm to warn the sleeping family.

In many ways the appliance control is the easiest and most impressive of talents to be exercised by the home computer. All the technology is in place; it is only a matter of economics and this will be no problem once the market is there.

GAMES

Solitaire games or those played with several friends grouped around a single display and keyboard will probably be stored in the home computer memory. We have seen those that are already available for the typical small computer. Suppose your computer now had a much larger memory or had access to that of a time-sharing computer. What games might be played?

If you don't mind crowding around the screen, you can play *Monopoly* on a hobby-sized computer today. *Chance* and *Community Chest* cards are randomized, and the computer throws the dice and keeps track of your finances. It doesn't handle side deals and auctions too well, but that will always be an exclusively human enterprise.

There are good *Checkers* programs. *Yahtzee* and a number

of other satisfactorily complex simulation games are available. In *Star Trader* players move space ships from star system to star system buying raw materials and selling manufactured goods, then selling the raw materials and buying other manufactured goods from more advanced planets. The costs of travel, the dangers of space storms and time warps, and the competitive pressure when another trader gets to your destination before you make this a challenging game that can go on for hours.

Chess programs have long been the favorite of dedicated computer hobbyists. The perfect chess strategy will probably never be devised. It would require searching through all possible sequences of moves before making a new move. So programmers use algorithms to limit the search to the most likely moves and only a few moves "deep"—into the future. The best chess programs are matched against each other in program tournaments. With due allowance for the usual disasters that attend these affairs (switches don't switch, lights don't light, and computers don't travel half so well as wine), the tournaments are often interesting events which demonstrate the ingenuity of the hobbyists as logical thinkers more than as programmers or even chess players.

For cryptologists there are programs that encode the alphabet so that secret messages can be sent and received. You can also use the computer to decipher the code and turn it into a difficult game. Of course if you are a spy, this is not just for fun but an essential part of your profession, and you probably know a lot more about it than the rest of us.

You can also encode a message in Morse code for radio transmission or translate a received and recorded Morse transmission into English. Ham radio operators have an affinity for computers, and many use the computer to search, record, and send their radio messages.

While the next couple of programs are not really games, I still think of them as entertainment. There is considerable controversy over biorhythm as a measure of the state of mind, emotions, and body, but the analysis is so easily programmed and the simplistic view of life so appealing it is difficult to resist a glance at your chart now and then. The theory states that at birth we all start at the midpoint of three cycles which are variously 33 days long (mental), 28 days long (emotional), and 23 days long (physical). We are more energetic, sharper, and emotionally happier during the upper halves of these cycles,

```
CHART SYMBOLS:
   P = 23-DAY PHYSICAL CYCLE
   E = 28-DAY EMOTIONAL OR SENSITIVITY CYCLE
   C = 33-DAY COGNITIVE (THINKING) OR CREATIVITY CYCLE
   * = SHOWS TWO OR THREE CYCLES AT SAME POINT

A CRITICAL TIME OCCURS
WHENEVER A CYCLE CROSSES THE MEDIAN LINE.
SOME PEOPLE BELIEVE YOU SHOULD BE ESPECIALLY CAREFUL THEN.


                         MINUS      MEDIAN      PLUS
     FRI   1 SEP 1978   E                •                PC
     SAT   2             E                •            P  C
     SUN   3               E              •          P  C
     MON   4                 E            •  P       C
     TUE   5                     E   P  •     C
     WED   6                     P   E  •C
     THU   7                 P      /   CE
     FRI   8               P          C   •    E
     SAT   9             P          C     •        E
     SUN  10           P          C       •           E
     MON  11           P        C         •              E
     TUE  12           P   C               •              E
     WED  13               •               •               E
     THU  14           C   P               •                E
     FRI  15           C         P         •                E
     SAT  16           C             P     •                E
     SUN  17           C                 P •               E
     MON  18            C                  •   P        E
     TUE  19              C                •        P E
     WED  20               C               •      E  P
     THU  21                 C             •  E         P
     FRI  22                   C           • E              P
     SAT  23                     C    E    •                 P
     SUN  24                     •    •                      P
     MON  25                   E    C                       P
     TUE  26               E              •  C           P
     WED  27             E                •      C   P
     THU  28           E                  •       P C
     FRI  29         E                    •  P          C
     SAT  30         E                P  •               C
                     E            P        •                C
                       E    P             •                  C
```

less energetic and productive during the lower halves. We are particularly vulnerable when the cycles cross the median from upper to lower or lower to upper. A typical printout of a biorhythm chart appears on page 212.

A biorhythm program is the simplest of the fortune-reading programs. It is only a step, though a fairly lengthy one, from biorhythms to *I Ching* and astrology. Like biorhythms, *I Ching* is entirely deterministic; that is, you throw coins or sticks six times, and the way they fall is interpreted as mathematical patterns that direct you to specific readings. These are supposed to suggest answers to the questions you were concentrating on as you threw the sticks. These readings are translated from the ancient Chinese Oracle—no outside expert or interpreter is necessary.

I Ching on a computer permits "throws" to be made by the user in a similarly random way. A "throw" consists of starting the random number generator through a sequence of fast-changing patterns. The sequence is stopped at the touch of the RETURN button which establishes each throw. The throw is therefore under your control but not your conscious control. The computer then looks up the appropriate reading and prints it out on your screen.

Astrology is not quite so deterministic and takes somewhat more elaborate programming, but much is already done. Astrological analysis by computer is being offered by several companies at low cost. They give you dozens of pages of computer printout based on your birthdate, time, and location. The mathematical data and the various conjunctions of planets are easily run on a computer. Precisely what these mean is better left to the experts.

In all of the games we have considered up to now the computer has been either the puzzle master or the opponent, but with time-sharing and multiple users the computer can also function as referee in games between humans. If both you and a friend have terminals in your respective homes, the computer can be your communications link. When you want to play a game of chess, for example, you sign on and ask for an opponent. The computer will scan its files for other users registered as chess players, and it can even choose one of comparable skill. It will call the other player to set a time for the game. When you are both ready to play, it displays the board on your terminal screen. First, you call out your move using normal chess notation. Then the computer changes the board accordingly and asks for your opponent's move. The computer will not permit illegal moves, and it will count time for each player if it is a timed game.

Similarly, you can set up a bridge game with four players, each in his own home, perhaps in cities very distant from each other. What a boon to the bedridden and to people in remote areas. The computer will shuffle the deck, deal the cards, record the bids, list the plays, and show each player his own hand and the table. It will keep score according to whatever system the players prefer and list the results at the end of the session or whenever called for. The computer does the chores and leaves the strategy making and excitement to the players.

LEARNING AT HOME

There are a number of games that have considerable educational value. We described the simulation games available for home computers in the last chapter—*Startrek*, *Kingdom*, and *Lem* in particular. Larger simulations are also available for hobby-sized computers and time-sharing systems and many more are being written. You can steer a ship, sail a boat, drive in traffic or on a racecourse, fly a jet plane, invest in stocks, or run a fictitious company on a computer.

For many years now the American Management Association as well as several business schools have offered computer simulations of business. Teams of executives are considered directors of competing manufacturing companies. They make normal business decisions—the price of a product, how many to manufacture in any particular time period, how to invest in production equipment, advertising, promotion, and so on. The decisions are entered into the simulation program, and the computer then prints out financial statements that tell each team how it did in the previous three months. The teams make a second set of decisions; the decisions are entered, and another three-month statement is printed out. After two or three game "years" a winner is declared but, more important, a discussion takes place which examines why one particular set of decisions was more successful than another. If experience is the best teacher, then this pseudo experience has to be second best, leaving books and theory much farther down the list.

Simulation games on social, political, agricultural, and ecological subjects are wonderful ways to study these subjects. All the freedom of human interaction is retained. The computer acts only as the referee and scorekeeper. It makes few if any value judgments.

Simulations are already in widespread use among high schools and colleges in subjects that are complex and intensely human. However, we shouldn't overlook the more straightforward programs that are also offered for college- and high-school-level study. At Dartmouth and at the University of Illinois there are hundreds of teaching programs on its computers, many of which are required "reading" for students of matheatics, science, history, language, and engineering. When their course material is essentially made up of facts which can be presented in a logical manner, it is simpler and more convenient to program the material and let the student acquire the data at his own speed. Large class lectures can then be replaced with seminars in which the students interact with the instructor and each other to explore the subtleties not easily programmed. College professors welcome the freedom from boring lectures (in which "the notes of the professor are transmitted to the notes of the students without passing through the minds of either") and are excited by the stimulation that head-to-head student-teacher confrontations provide.

It may be more informative to list the kinds of high school and college courses that are *not* adaptable to computer-aided instruction. The creative arts immediately come to mind—writing, music, and art require a continual feedback from teacher to student of a more qualitative kind than can be programmed on computers. Philosophy, psychology, and political science have aspects that are best taught in a seminar environment with live instructors.

Testing is another part of schoolwork that programs easily. Multiple-choice tests have been graded by computers for some time. However, it is still rare to have the test administered by the computer. Scholastic achievement tests for college entrance and examinations for course grades couldn't be done on the home terminal or computer because of the opportunity to cheat. Nevertheless terminals in school could be proctored as easily as written examinations are today.

I.Q. tests, personality tests, career preference tests, and even some college entrance tests could be taken at home and graded at once—no more waiting. College admissions offices could prepare their own tests and administer them to new applicants while they were waiting to be interviewed.

Many popularized personality tests are self-administered as much for entertainment as anything else. Are you an introvert or an extrovert? Can you live with a liberated woman? What kind of husband (wife) would you find most compatible? These kinds of tests will be available on cassettes or through time-sharing to run on your home terminal.

BUSINESS AND FINANCE

Hundreds of programs written for small business computers adapt easily to the home environment. Inventory control takes care of the pantry. Payroll and tax programs help with income taxes. Accounts payable and receivable do the bills. General ledger handles the budget. Stock portfolio analysis advises on investments. Depreciation calculations apply to the house and car. Lease/purchase decisions are similar whether they are in hundreds or millions of dollars. As we saw with the bank statement program in the last chapter the home computer can do on a daily basis what the bank or outside consultant does only monthly or yearly.

Computers now list all telephone calls and automatically bill you at the end of the month. Electricity, oil, and gas fuel usage are read on your meter manually, but all billing calculations are done by computer. I expect that even the readings will eventually be sent automatically to the central billing office.

Supermarkets are installing optical systems to read the Universal Product Code pattern for checkout and inventory control. The black line pattern tells price, product name, manufacturer, and quantity. The price is rung up on the register, and the store inventory is adjusted so that the manager can control his stock much more efficiently. Then, to pay for the items we purchase, most of us write a check and wait for an OK of our credit rating. Then the supermarket deposits the check in its bank account. It would be much simpler if we could authorize our own bank to deduct the purchase from our own account and add it to the supermarket's in one quick transaction.

This is the promised "checkless" society, and it is well within our technical capabilities. Banks couldn't function today without computer control of account balances, interest calculations, and check clearances. Tellers already access the bank data base while you wait for your deposit receipt or cash withdrawal. It saves much time and effort when other terminals in stores and at your place of employment automatically credit or debit your account. Obviously foolproof security is necessary in the form of an identification card or code word which only you would know, but this is certainly feasible.

One real disadvantage of the checkless society is that we lose our "float." Right now there is a delay of a day or two and perhaps as much as a week to ten days from the time you write a check to the time the money is actually deducted from your bank account. With immediate cash transfer you won't be able to "cover" your check a week after it has been written. But I expect that banks, which already offer credit cards of their own, will allow overdrafts with little or no surcharge. Visa and Master Charge effectively extend free credit for a minimum of 30 days. Why shouldn't their parent banks do the same? In this way your bank account and credit account are combined. Habitual deadbeats need not apply.

THE ELECTRONIC POST OFFICE

A society that functions well without paper checks can also function without paper mail. All communications, business and personal, can be handled by time-sharing computers. Letters, memoranda, notes, invitations, greeting cards would be prepared by text-handling systems in the personal computer and sent down the cable to the central computer. There they would be routed to the proper address and held in a "mail" file for the recipients until they are ready to read it.

You will type (eventually just talk) into the computer and it will prepare an error-free, beautifully formatted letter for the screen or printer of the addressee. You can leave notes for your family or for the milkman, and they'll be printed out to the properly identified person in the house or announced from the speaker at the kitchen door. The computer would keep a record of the fact that the message had been delivered and hold the reply, if any.

Time-sharing opens a whole communications network separate from, or in addition to, our telephone network. Already communication satellites are relaying data and messages across the Atlantic Ocean by microwave radio signals needing no cable. Very soon a small microwave "dish" in your attic will be all that is necessary to connect you with any telephone or computer terminal in the world.

A programmable computer as the central switchboard creates a new dimension in interpersonal communication. One dull Friday evening a young, single woman may come home from work and face an empty apartment and an empty evening. She will sit at her terminal and type, "I want to talk to a single man, aged 30 to 35, who lives in this locality and likes French cooking." The computer will check its user list, and when it finds such a man who wants to respond it will connect the two so that they may type messages to each other.

Call them pen pals or computer dates or simply lonely people; the computer will help them find each other and offer them the opportunity to talk with total anonymity and security. They can be Tarzan and Jane or Superman and Earth Mother to each other. They can say the most outrageous things, cut off or out, call again at a later time, make a date, fall in love, marry, or never talk again. They can reveal their deepest secrets and pretend to fictional secrets. They can be imaginative or dull. No one will monitor their conversation, and neither need ever know that the person they talked to last night now sits next to them on the bus or works at a desk across the aisle.

INFORMATION

Think of the computer memory as an immense library. Magnetic disks spin at thousands of revolutions per minute and store millions of words, all properly coded, in bits and bytes. Instead of climbing around stacks of magazines or books to find a particular article, you call it up on your screen. Type in an accession number and the computer prints out title, author, date of publication, place of publication. If you like, it will print an abstract of the article. If you want the entire original it will display it on your screen, page by page or paragraph by paragraph.

Knowing what we do about computers and memories, we can see how practical this is. Reading for pleasure is still not comfortable on the screen with the tube face only 12 or 15 inches from your nose. It is certainly not practical at $10 or more per hour when you can buy a paperback book for $1.95. But reference and research material are very economically searched through a time-sharing computer because the computer has immense storage capacity plus a mechanized and logical search capability.

Here is how it works. Just about every article and book published in the English language today, and many in foreign languages, has been already read and digested by professional editors. They are paid to do it for science, for industry, for government researchers who need the information. The editors write four or five sentences describing what is in the article and then select from a prepared list of index terms the subject areas referred to in the article. Source, publisher, date, and all the other usual bibliographic information are added to the digest. The summary is then typed into a computer file and becomes part of the data base.

Now suppose you want information on a particular subject—it could be for entertainment, business, professional, or home use. You start the search routine by typing in the most logical subject that describes what you want. The computer looks through its file of "descriptors"—the words the editor used to describe the contents of the article—and then simply counts up the number of "hits." Perhaps it finds 400 digests that have been indexed under the term you used. Obviously that is too many for convenient reading. You are not likely to want to read 400 digests any more than you would want to read all 400 original articles. So you pick another related subject that may cut down the number of hits. Type that in and maybe you will find you are in even more trouble. Suppose there are 600 digests in the file indexed under the new term.

Take a real example to see how it works. You think the television game you bought is producing a poor image on your television set and that it may be caused by the radio frequency modulator in the video game. If you were to go to the library with your problem, you would first find an index to periodicals in the electrical and electronic fields, where information of this kind is likely to have been published. You look in that index under "television," "games," "video," or "modulator." Under each heading you find a list of article titles and by scanning these you hope eventually to find a good reference. Then you go back to the librarian and ask for the particular issue of the indicated publication. You take it to a table, read it, make notes, or make a copy on the copying machine in the library. This takes a couple of hours at least plus travel time to the library.

Now let's search it "online." It's the same procedure we used to find a dinner menu, only this time applied to a much larger literature. You sign on to the time-sharing network from your home terminal. The list of data bases appears on the screen and you pick the one for electronics. You type:

SELECT TELEVISION

The answer comes back:

SET	SUBJECT	ITEMS
1	TELEVISION	8221

Which means there are 8,221 articles indexed under "television" in the data base. You try another selection:

SELECT VIDEO

SET	SUBJECT	ITEMS
1	TELEVISION	8221
2	VIDEO	2959

which is better, though not much. Let's keep going:

```
SELECT GAMES

SET    SUBJECT         ITEMS
 1     TELEVISION      8221
 2     VIDEO           2959
 3     GAMES           1005
```

Still better, but now let's use the logical "and" to find those items which include both video and games in their digests:

```
COMBINE 2 AND 3

SET    SUBJECT         ITEMS
 1     TELEVISION      8221
 2     VIDEO           2959
 3     GAMES           1005
 4     2 AND 3           10
```

That's more like it. There are only 10 articles on video games. You now ask to see the titles of the 10 articles:

```
PRINT TITLES SET 4
```

The computer responds:

1. VIDEO GAMES BY GRUNDIG (GERMAN)
2. MICROGAME
3. AN INTEGRATED TV VIDEO MODULATION SYSTEM
4. THE HISTORY OF VIDEO GAMES
5. ACTIVE TELEVISION WITH VIDEO GAMES
6. BUILD THIS GREAT TV GAME
7. BUILD YOUR OWN VIDEO BALLGAME
8. MORE COMPLEX VIDEO GAMES KEEP PLAYER INTEREST HIGH
9. A TELEVISION GAME DEVICE
10. LSI CHIPS TAKING OVER MORE HOUSEHOLD CHORES

There it is, number 3. You ask for a digest:

PRINT DIGEST ITEM 3

NEW DEVELOPMENTS IN TV ADD-ON AREAS SUCH AS
VDR, GAMES, AND DATA DISPLAY HAVE PRODUCED A
COMMON NEED FOR COMPOSITE VIDEO ENCODING
AND RF MODULATION CIRCUITS TO INTERFACE WITH
THE TV RECEIVER. THIS PAPER REVIEWS THE BASIC
REQUIREMENTS FOR THIS AREA AND THEN
PRESENTS A NEW TV VIDEO MODULATION SYSTEM
USING ONLY ONE INTEGRATED CIRCUIT. THE NEW
SYSTEM INCLUDES THE SOUND SUBCARRIER
OSCILLATOR AND CHROMA SUBCARRIER ENCODING
CIRCUITS IN ADDITION TO RF OSCILLATOR AND
MODULATOR FOR TWO LOW-VHF CHANNELS.
CHANNEL SWITCHING IS ACHIEVED WITH A
DC-OPERATED SWITCH.

The title, author, date, and source of publication follow.

Perhaps this article is a little too technical for your taste but it is essentially what you wanted. You look up the source reference and, with the touch of a button, order a copy to be mailed to you or be printed out at your terminal. Total elapsed time: perhaps ten minutes. Total cost at current prices—$13.48. No carfare, no gasoline wasted, no parking expense at the library garage.

Well over a hundred such data bases are currently available at your terminal. Industry and government are the largest users, but there is no reason the average home computer couldn't hook into the same system. Most have no minimum fee; you pay for what you use. And once there are enough of us accessing the electronic library, costs will be much lower. When it will only cost a few cents to go to the electronic library research will become a joyful exploration for all of us.

THE ELECTRONIC NEWSPAPER

What is it that the newspaper offers that a library doesn't? The answer is currency. The newspaper tells us today's news, sports results, stock market quotations, weather report. The advertisements inform us of new merchandise and sales, the supermarkets tell us about specials and food prices, the classified ads tell us what is available today in goods or services, apartments or job openings. Isn't all that perfect for the computer data bank?

Newspapers are already trapped between television for up-to-the-minute news and news magazines for in-depth analysis or special interest. The time-sharing computer attacks them in their last haven. Daily listings are much more efficiently read on the time-sharing terminal. The full stock market report needn't be printed out at your terminal—only those companies of interest to you. The full sports results needn't be printed out—only those sports and teams that you follow. All of the real estate ads or the help wanted or the automobiles-for-sale classified sections needn't be printed at your terminal—just those sections that you are concerned with.

When you read an ad that you want to follow up, you can phone the advertiser or write a message on the terminal to be held in his "mailbox." It's fast and saves paper, postage, and telephone costs.

Newspaper classified ads are a natural for the time-sharing network, but so are a lot of other things. Supermarket ads are important to a lot of us who keep tabs on our food bills. The supermarket manager will call in the information on Wednesday night in much the same way he does now, but instead of having to buy and save the Thursday morning paper a shopper will have all week to scan listings on the terminal screen.

Eventually all the marketing can be done from the terminal. After selecting your groceries from the listings, you put your order in at the terminal. The supermarket will pick the products in their proper quantities and bag and deliver them to your kitchen door in a couple of hours.

The same thing is true for almost all household shopping. You can call the butcher's computer and place your order there. The wine shop could list its stock on your terminal when you call in and take your order then and there.

Anything you would buy from a catalog—books, records, appliances, even hardware and drapes and rugs—could as easily be purchased at the terminal. When pictures and color are added to these transmissions—and they will, though it may be a few years—the service will be as personalized as any shopping you now do in the store.

It won't replace all shopping, of course. A lot of the fun of shopping comes from roaming through stores, looking at different styles, touching the fabrics, turning the knobs. But wouldn't you rather skip the hunting for basic necessities that just take time?

What other unique services do newspapers provide? Even coming events like movie, theater, sports, and television program listings can be updated daily on the computer data bank. The listings would be indexed by type of entertainment, subject matter, locality, and a review could be appended. You can scan for something to do as easily on the screen as you can through last Sunday's newspaper.

It's not hard to see newspapers replaced by terminals, is it?

THE ELECTRONIC DOCTOR, LAWYER, SENATOR

Hospitals were fairly quick to put their patients' records on the computer. Today when you enter some hospitals, the registration procedure has you directly answering the questions at a computer terminal or has a volunteer doing it for you. All medications, test results, orders written by the doctor, and observations made by the nurses are recorded on your electronic record.

Just as the data bank can hold articles from newspapers or magazines, it can also hold the literature of medicine and law.

But the medical literature has been indexed and combined in a far more sophisticated way. It is now possible for a doctor to type in a set of symptoms and other medical test results and get out one or more tentative diagnoses. Lacking enough data the computer can indicate what further tests would be necessary to confirm a diagnosis and what the prescribed course of treatment might be. Doctors can't possibly keep up to date while they are treating patients eight or ten hours a day. The electronic medical library can be of great assistance without in any way reducing personal attention. If anything, it should free doctors from unending study to devote more time to patients.

Law libraries have also been put into data banks. The literature is enormous, and the task of encoding and indexing all decisions and judgments is probably impossible. But laws as written and enacted can certainly be programmed, and eventually they will be analyzed by the logic of the computer to prevent the contradictions or absurdities that occasionally occur.

Politicians may not take kindly to the computer for a very good reason: someday you may vote from your computer terminal and put a lot of politicians out of jobs. Representational government is no longer a necessity. What we continue to need are lawmakers. Once every six months or so proposed legislation can be put to the entire electorate for its approval. A few minutes at the terminal will count your vote along with those of every other registered voter in the population. In effect every law is submitted to a referendum. Why not?

CREATIVE ART

We talked earlier about writing music with the home computer. It can relieve the composer of the need to be a performer or to be tied down to the limitations of a particular instrument. Similarly, programming can replace painting technique, at least of the nonrepresentational kind. A computer will never create a Degas dancer or a Rembrandt portrait, but computers can be the canvas of much of the nonobjective art we see today. With higher-level languages and more sophisticated programs, computers will actually write the music and paint the pictures called up by instructions that ask for the mood, tempo, perhaps the richness of music or art. The computer can generate melody, choose key, provide harmony and instrumentation, and, of course, perform the work.

A color "painting" might be re-created on a wall-sized screen that hangs in your living room. You call for mood, tempo, color, and quality of line, and the computer would choose, under the control of a random generator, the burst of color and style that seems appropriate.

Computers have already written poetry from a given vocabulary and produced language and imagery free from many of the built-in limitations that humans have. Trained for years in the "proper" use of language, poets struggle to break away from clichés of language and idea that computers know nothing of.

EPILOG

From the moment we are born and the details entered into the hospital computer—through schooling, job, taxes, brushes with traffic policemen, insurance companies, Social Security, banks, credit cards, mortgage loans, grocery and department store shopping; at play or at work, in the arts or the sciences—the computer stays with us as recording secretary, teacher, diagnostician, protector, and playmate.

What can it be used for? *The Economist* answers, "What are the applications of electricity?"

It is traditional to start articles on the future by portraying a day in the life of Mr. Ordinary American in the year 2000. I will move it up ten years, to 1990, and end this book with a scenario of my own. We know a lot about life in 1990. For the most part people, their homes, their cars will look much the same as they do today. Clothes styles, hair styles, and automobile bodies will be a little different but no more unusual than an early sixties car or dress or suit looks today. The real differences will be in the electric signals that run through the wires in our homes and in the radio signals that fill the air around us.

There will be upward of 50,000,000 computers in American homes—still only half as many homes that have color television today. The computer will be a box the size and weight of a stereo receiver. It will be tucked away in a closet or in the basement with the other service equipment and plugged into the standard 110-volt house current outlet. On the top surface of the computer box there will be a small dish antenna aimed at a communications satellite hanging in the sky above. There will be five or six terminals in the home—in the kitchen, bedrooms, study, and family room. The terminals will communicate with the computer and, through it, to the outside world. There will be no outside telephone lines, no television antenna. The television sets in the house will get their signals from the computer.

As our scene opens dawn is breaking on a cold January day.

7:03:26 A.M.   The light night snow was melted by heating coils embedded in the cement walks and, sensing that the pavement is now dry, the computer cuts off the warming current. The house has been kept at an energy-saving 18 degrees (Celsius, of course) all night. Now it is time to warm things up a bit. The furnace is turned up, and it will maintain the temperature at 22 degrees until the family is in bed that night. It takes about half an hour to warm the house to the new setting.

7:30:00 A.M.   Soft music comes from the speaker near the bedroom terminal. It is John's favorite melody written and arranged by a program mixed accidentally into the music generator from a tax subroutine John was using last April. Slowly the tempo and volume increase until the sound insinuates itself into his dream and then to his conscious mind. He awakens, and as he rises from the bed the music shifts to a lively but unintrusive popular hit of the day.

"OK, I'm up," John says aloud. The bedroom speakers become quiet, and the weather and news are announced by the speaker over the bathroom mirror as John shaves and showers.

John is a morning person, and his mind is abuzz with plans and ideas that he thought of during the night. He wraps a bathrobe around his still damp shoulders and sits at the desk console in the adjoining study. First, he dictates a series of short notes to himself which will be printed out and left on his office desk when he gets there later in the morning. Then he makes several changes in his calendar and to two stored job files. While there he decides to scan his incoming mail. Memos, notes, and letters collected overnight appear one by one on the screen. John dictates responses to three, discards a couple, bucks two to other executives in his company, and holds two for a meeting that is scheduled for later that morning. He checks his calendar for the day and sees he is to meet with the company president in a few minutes, so he signs off and finishes dressing.

8:05:41 A.M.   Jane gets out of bed as John heads downstairs to the kitchen. She hears the bath being filled for her as she runs through a brief series of calisthenics called out by the bedroom speaker.

John finds the coffee ready, of course. The built-in drip appliance was started as he entered the shower. He takes two retort trays from a shelf in the kitchen cabinet and tosses them into the microwave oven. In ten seconds the door pops open. He fishes out the hot little trays, peels off the covers, and takes the scrambled eggs and toast to the breakfast nook table. John scans the morning headlines on the terminal screen there but eats quickly and with scant attention since he is thinking about his upcoming meeting with the boss.

He goes out the back door to the car (the engine is running and warm) and drives the short distance to his suburban office. He knows it is old-fashioned to keep the office rather than let everyone work from home, but he enjoys the personal contact with the other company executives and the president, and he is also grateful that it takes him away from home. With Jane home all day he thinks they would soon get on each other's nerves if they both worked from the house.

8:27:52 A.M.   Jane is soaking happily in the hot bath but decides she needs to get the household chores done early this morning. She wraps the big towel around her slim body and sits at the study console. She searches her recipe list to decide on the menu for the dinner they are giving that evening for four friends. Having settled on the dishes to be served, she calls for an ingredients list which is automatically sorted by the store type. She runs the ingredients against her pantry inventory and finds that there are very few things she will have to buy for the dinner—just veal and the wine.

She checks her bank account to see the current balance. There are three items not deducted yet because she had put a hold on them until an outstanding commission has been deposited. She notes with satisfaction that the commission came in during the night, so she releases the held items and calls the butcher and liquor store to place her orders. As an afterthought she adds brandy to the wine list which she knows John will be pleased to offer to their guests after dinner.

9:15:32 A.M.   Jane hears the vacuum cleaner working its way around the living room as she gets her own breakfast—juice from the refrigerator spout and coffee from the still-hot coffeemaker. She takes her vitamin tablet and resolves to fast until dinner with her guests that evening. She calls in a calendar entry to get her started dressing at 6:30 P.M. and asks for a soft chime at 8:00 P.M. so that she will be reminded to start cooking then.

She checks Jack on the monitor and is pleased to see that he is awake and already well into his calculus program. Jack is a bright fifteen-year-old who has already finished all the prescribed high school courses and is well into the college level material he will need for the business degree he wants. He has been racing through the math and science programs so fast that Jane was concerned that he wasn't keeping the material, but John assures her that he is, based on his conversations with the boy.

Jill is playing a marathon commodities game with three friends (two in the next town, one across the state), and Jane decides to interrupt her with a reminder that morning is for school work, not games. She presses the message button and says, "Games later, sweetheart. There's a civics course that needs some attention right now."

The message will appear on Jill's screen at the next convenient break point. Only *she* will see it because it is a private family communication.

10:09:11 A.M.   Coffee cup in hand, Jane ducks past the vacuum cleaner which is now coming out of the bedroom and sits at the desk in the study. Jane runs a small firm that sells real estate to corporations. It's all plants and warehouses these days; no new offices or office buildings have gone up in the area in three years—which is not surprising since so much administrative work is done out of homes these days. All new corporate buildings are windowless blocks generously surrounded by green bushes and trees so that they won't be eyesores. Real estate zoning has become so complicated that Jane has a special file in her computer just to keep track of which tracts of land are zoned in which way. She is very pleased to be out of the residential house-hunting market which took many hours walking potential buyers through homes. Businessmen are more concerned with statistics on traffic flow, availability and cost of power, transportation, and the local tax situation than they are with the color of the roof or what flowers are planted in the backyard.

Before making her first call of the day Jane checks her biorhythms. The graphs appear on her screen, and she notes with relief that she is past that nasty double critical point. Both mental and emotional graphs are now well above the midline, but she has to be careful with her body which is in the lower half of its cycle. She looks forward to a good week. She also checks John's chart (he doesn't believe in it but she finds it helpful in predicting his moods as well as those of the children). Then she takes a quick look at the astrological forecasts for both of them. They subscribed to the Zodiac three years earlier, and she finds, and John agrees, that the interpretations of their personalities and relationship are amazingly accurate but not too good on day-to-day activities.

Her first order of business is to call a new client to get his specifications. He is vaguer than most. Gently she leads him through her checklist—square footage, price range, what he plans to use the space for, pollution standards he can live up to, whether he will be shipping by air or truck, the kinds of materials that will be coming in, and the sort of finished packages that will be going out, and so on. As he gives his answers she keys them into her program and runs the data against her listings.

Her first preference is listings handled by her company exclusively. Second is the two other real estate firms she works most closely with. Her third choice is open listings offered by any other firm or private sellers. After the first couple of specification entries, she can see that there will be few qualified listings. By the end of the checklist she finds only two parcels of land that will do. She holds the price specification until the last because this is traditionally the toughest one to meet and the one most easily modified if the property is desirable enough.

Sure enough, she enters his price range and the two remaining parcels are knocked out. She backs off the price limitation and says to the client, "I have two properties for you," and then goes into her usual sales pitch. She puts the two plans on the screen for him and reviews the data about locality, roads and highways nearby, and what he can hope for in tax preferences in each of the two townships. He records the data on his own computer file for study and discussion with his staff, groans at the asking prices, and wonders how negotiable they may be. Jane thinks there is some give if he comes up with a good offer and they sign off.

11:46:29 A.M.   As she flicks the voice phone switch and logs off the real estate program, a message appears on the screen:

```
MOM. WE ARE GOING BIKE RIDING. SEE YOU
LATER.—11:02:15
```

The back door slams and Jane assumes it must be their cleaning woman. That's a relief. With guests coming this evening Jane didn't want to get tied up in housecleaning. There isn't much that needs to be done. Except for special dinners they take most of their meals out of retort packages or the freezer. The dishwasher takes care of the rest. Fresh meat is a treat they all like but more trouble than they are usually willing to take, given how little time they spend at the dinner table. So there are few pans or grills to clean.

The cleaning woman dusts, mops the kitchen, cleans the bathrooms, and does the laundry. She comes two afternoons a week, and both Jane and John find it necessary to do some work around the house every day.

OK, back to work. Her small business runs easily on the home computer. She has two assistants and all they do is sell. If she had to pay a secretary, bookkeeper, tax consultant, and office manager she couldn't make a profit. Jane runs the payroll program for herself and her two employees which takes their salaries and commissions and calculates their net pay. She hasn't run the old check-writing program for over a year now that their pay is deposited directly into their accounts. Tax deductions are automatically deposited in a separate account she maintains with the I.R.S. She runs the general profit statement and notes with some pleasure that while costs have risen with the salary increases, sales went up even more. She prints out trend lines month by month, does a quick check on country-wide and local sales trends, and can see that overall sales will hold up well during the next six months. Since her share of the local market has been increasing, her operating profits should more than double this year.

Jane logs off the business program and decides to reward herself with a cup of coffee. She goes down to the kitchen, tells the cleaning woman that there will be four guests for dinner that evening, and asks her to set the table before she leaves.

1:15:09 P.M.   The children come romping in just as she settles down to what was going to be a quiet moment of introspection in the breakfast nook. They pop frozen hot dogs into the microwave oven, take milk from the refrigerator spout, and race up to their rooms for the afternoon television shows. Apparently Jack has a bet with a friend on a basketball game being broadcast live in Houston. Jill is learning to program a plastic-molding machine which Jane only vaguely understands. Three-dimensional images are projected into a transparent cube following the instructions the operator writes. She has done several swirling shapes of brilliant color but is now trying a portrait of her father's head, and this is proving a lot more difficult.

So Jane gets her few minutes of quiet after all. She scans the classified listings on the kitchen screen, idly looking for a secondhand music synthesizer. She believes the children's music education is being neglected and that if they could program some music of their own with more than the four voices their home computer can handle, they might take more interest. She also checks the department store sale listings to see if the dish pattern she wants has been reduced. It has and Jane types in an order for eight five-piece place settings. The department store computer assures her the dishes are in stock and will be delivered that afternoon.

Then remembering the very encouraging profit projections for the rest of the business year, she calls up the fur department and lets the salesperson (who is sitting in her own home) flash coat model sequences on her screen. The terminal screen isn't adequate to show the detail in these pictures, but Jane gets some sense of the styles and colors now in fashion. The prices, of course, are incredible. She decides to stop by and look in person on her way back from the real estate site she will be visiting that afternoon. Coffee done, she goes upstairs to get dressed.

2:05:55 P.M.   Jane leaves by the back door to the garage. The cleaning woman will be leaving in a couple of hours, and since the children have gone to visit friends, the house will soon be empty. Jane stops at the kitchen terminal on the way out and says, "Take messages."

4:30:15 P.M.   The cleaning woman puts her coat on in the kitchen and presses the security button just before going out the door. Front and rear door deadbolts snick into place and the alarm system is activated. Now any motion detected within the house will immediately set off a loud alarm both inside and outdoors, and the automatic dialer will call the local police station. The fire detection system is always activated whether the house is occupied or not. This will sound loud alarms and, if not deactivated within five minutes, the telephone will dial the fire station.

The burglar alarm surrounding the house is more subtle. It has microphone pickups embedded in the brick walls and the concrete foundation so that any unusual sounds like tapping at the doors or scratching or breaking of glass are detected and compared to normal household sounds. If the frequency spectrum of the new sound is substantially different, it indicates an unusual event is taking place. If the house is occupied, the speakers will announce the event. If it is unoccupied, the police will be notified and the alarms sounded.

And so the house is quiet. The temperature is held at the daytime setting. Three phone calls are answered and the messages recorded.

5:15:18 P.M. Jane calls in from her car and takes the recorded phone messages. Normally all phone calls are automatically forwarded to her car, but her order to take messages disabled the forwarding circuit and the computer answered.

Jack rides his bike into the garage. The computer system detects the sounds correctly, interprets them as safe, and holds reaction. He sets the bike in the stand and as he approaches the back door shouts, "It's me!"

He isn't supposed to do it that way. The correct identifier is his full name, spoken clearly and closer to the door so that echoes and other noises will not be mixed in. But the computer has recorded his frequency and time spectrum often enough so that he knows it will work. It does. The bolt is drawn and the door swings open.

Jack dials up the pantry inventory on the kitchen screen and decides on a piece of chocolate cake with ice cream. He wants to eat it before his Mom gets home and chides him about ruining his appetite for dinner.

Cake and ice cream are in the freezer individually wrapped in single-portion sizes. He pops the cake into the microwave oven for 15 seconds and puts the ice cream in for 2 seconds because he likes it soft. It runs thickly as he pours it over the cake. Halfway through the cake Jill comes in and nibbles the crumbs around his plastic dish. They finish and go to their rooms to watch television.

6:18:48 P.M. John has to pause briefly in the car outside the garage to wait for the door to open. It has been reacting a little slowly this week, and he is convinced that there is something wrong with the antenna in the car transmitter. While none of the automatic warning lights are lit on the trouble panel, he can sense that the car needs service. All its responses are just a little more sluggish than he is accustomed to. It takes more effort on the brakes, the acceleration is slower, and, on the highways, the automatic steering isn't as tight as it was when he took delivery on the car six months earlier.

As he enters the kitchen the garage door closes and the lights go off. He talks his concerns about the car at the kitchen terminal so he won't forget, and an appointment is set up for him to drop the car off at the service station tomorrow. He'll be reminded of it when he checks his calendar in the morning.

"Who's home?" he asks. The computer answers, "Jack and Jill are in their rooms."

John shrugs in annoyance. Jane knows they have company tonight, and she'll spend two hours getting dressed while he has to entertain the first arrivals alone. He passes through the dining room and is pleased to see the table set, fresh flowers on the mantel, and three bottles of a decent wine on the sideboard. He goes up to shower and change.

6:46:22 P.M. Jane drives her little runabout into the recharge plug in the garage. She is pleased about the way the new guidance system takes care of the steering and stopping when she gets within six feet of the plug. No more complaints about broken plugs and scraped fenders. She sees that John is home already and rushes upstairs to get dressed.

Her bath is cold since it had been programmed for 6:30. Jane lets it drain while she strips out of her clothes and exchanges the day's events with John. As he leaves the bathroom Jane steps into the shower, tucking her shower cap tightly around her ears. By 7:30 they are both downstairs. The children have had dinner and are both in serious teen-age conversations with friends. John is filling the ice bucket and setting out the liquor; Jane is checking the menu, setting out the retort pouches that will be needed later, and running through the cooking schedule that has been printed out on the screen so that she will know approximately what is to be done when the chime sounds at 8:00. She decides to prepare the hollandaise at once and in the blender. It never fails and takes only 90 seconds to cook after the butter is melted and hot.

Five minutes later the computer announces, "Front door," and within a few seconds they hear the doorbell. John calls out, "Coming," and goes to the door. The door can be unlocked with a word, but for guests he still feels it is more gracious to open the door himself. Jane finishes the hollandaise, puts it in the warmer, and joins their guests.

8:00:00 P.M.   A soft chime sounds from the living room speaker, and Jane excuses herself and goes to the kitchen to get dinner. In ten minutes all the cold food is on the table. The appetizers are hot and ready. Jane calls her guests to the table and John pours the wine.

Jane heats the main course while she clears the appetizer plates. Later she clears the dinner plates, helped by a male guest who wants to discuss new zoning legislation with her privately in the kitchen. The group then lingers for some time over fruit, the rest of the wine, and the brandy. Jane had expected to serve a sweet dessert, but the mood was much too philosophical and the dinner too heavy.

11:19:35 P.M.   Their last guests leave with thanks. It is early, but they will all be busy the next morning in their separate professions. John clears the dishes and carries them to the dishwasher which scrapes, stacks, and washes them automatically. Upstairs Jane says, "Bedtime" into the terminal microphone. The downstairs lights turn off and the furnace thermostat is set down to 18 degrees. The door bolts lock and the burglar alarm is activated for the night.

Jane checks the children's rooms at the bedroom terminal. She wanted an infrared scanner, but John says it is an intrusion on the kids' privacy now that they are both teen-agers. All she hears are their radios, so she goes to their rooms and confirms that they are both in bed and asleep. She turns their radios down and joins John in their large double bed.

INDEX